T0156901

ENDORSEMENTS

"The Empty Front Porch is a wonderful book. With insouciance, humor, and first-rate story telling, Cynthia Mills provides a clarion call for a life that is truly worth living. While that would be more than enough, her book also provides a compelling workbook full of the experiential exercises that will turn your vocation into a way of life. If you are seeking a more meaningful life then read this book!"

> August Turak, author of *Business Secrets of the Trappist Monks*, Forbes.com contributor, entrepreneur, and speaker, www.augustturak.com

"Whether you are uncertain about your faith or well along in your journey, the insights Cynthia shares will cause you to pause, sit a while and stop the swirl of the world around you. Learn how silence can speak boldly and refresh your soul. Choose to walk up the porch steps, take your seat and accept a hand to co-create the life you are truly meant to live!"

> Barbara and Dave Zerfoss, authors of *The Power of Nothing, Stress is a Choice,* and *Stress Less and Enjoy Each Day,* www.TheZerfossGroup.com

"This is an eye-opening resource for Christians to evaluate their "porch". In today's busy world it is easy to lose focus of what is truly important. Take the time to sit with your soul and design your porch to Porch plan. Cynthia is a shining light for the Holy Spirit."

> Chip Eichelberger, co-author of *Smart Guide To Accomplishing Your Goals,* former Tony Robbins international point man, and NSA Certified Speaking Professional, www.GetSwitchedOn.com

— THE —
EMPTY FRONT
PORCH

Soul Sittin' to Design
Your porch to Porch Plan

CYNTHIA SPRAKER MILLS

WESTBOW°
PRESS
A DIVISION OF THOMAS NELSON
& ZONDERVAN

Scripture taken from the Holy Bible, NEW INTERNATIONAL VERSION®. Copyright ©
1973, 1978, 1984 by Biblica, Inc. All rights reserved worldwide. Used by permission. NEW
INTERNATIONAL VERSION® and NIV® are registered trademarks of Biblica, Inc. Use of either
trademark for the offering of goods or services requires the prior written consent of Biblica US, Inc.

Scripture quotations are from The Holy Bible, English Standard Version® (ESV®), copyright © 2001
by Crossway, a publishing ministry of Good News Publishers. Used by permission. All rights reserved.

Scripture taken from the New King James Version. Copyright © 1979, 1980,
1982 by Thomas Nelson, Inc. Used by permission. All rights reserved.

Scripture quotations taken from the New American Standard Bible®, Copyright
© 1960, 1962, 1963, 1968, 1971, 1972, 1973, 1975, 1977, 1995 by The
Lockman Foundation. Used by permission. (www.Lockman.org)

Scripture quotations taken from the Holy Bible, New Living Translation, Copyright © 1996, 2004.
Used by permission of Tyndale House Publishers, Inc., Wheaton, Illinois 60189. All rights reserved.

Scripture taken from the King James Version of the Bible.

Scripture taken from the Contemporary English Version © 1991, 1992,
1995 by American Bible Society, Used by Permission.

Some photos used were from Dreamstime.

WestBow Press books may be ordered through booksellers or by contacting:

WestBow Press
A Division of Thomas Nelson & Zondervan
1663 Liberty Drive
Bloomington, IN 47403
www.westbowpress.com
1 (866) 928-1240

ISBN: 978-1-4908-8185-0 (sc)
ISBN: 978-1-4908-8186-7 (hc)
ISBN: 978-1-4908-8184-3 (e)

Library of Congress Control Number: 2015908340

Print information available on the last page.

WestBow Press rev. date: 07/09/2015

TABLE OF CONTENTS

DEDICATION

Thirty years ago, two of my college friends were killed in separate car accidents exactly two months to the day apart – October 14 and December 14, 1984. One lit up the world with her spirit, smile, and infectious love of life. She was a giver and carried joy into any room, a blessing to others by simply being alive. The other was a woman who noticeably walked with God, whose intellect and business acumen were going to impact the corporate life of an up and coming city, and without a doubt was a leader in the making who would have helped to transform lives.

Both of these women knew how to have full front porches by the time they had lived barely two decades. Selfishly, I wish they had stayed on the earthly front porch longer, and no, I have no understanding of why that was not in the plan. How I would have loved to watch where God took their lives, but I know they were welcomed back to the Heavenly Front Porch with great anticipation.

I dedicate this book to my fellow Virginians, Queens College alums, and friends - Rosemary Kidd and Michelle Sluder. I've continued on the journey, made my mistakes, lived as fully as I have known how, and sought my Heavenly Father, whom you have both dwelt with now for most of my life. I look forward to seeing you in the welcome party when I return to the Heavenly Front Porch.

The author (right) front porch sittin' in the early years

"Do not conform to the pattern of this world, but be transformed by the renewing of your mind. Then you will be able to test and approve what God's will is – His good, pleasing and perfect will."[1]

INTRODUCTION

Some have soul clarity from childhood. I want to be a fireman, a nurse, a teacher, or an astronaut. Others' journeys unfold, and gifts are revealed along the way. God speaks in our experiences if we seek Him and listen for Him. Discovering our gifts and their best use is a daily act of humility and obedience. Choosing a life of service is a choice not to be in charge.

---

[1] Romans 12:2 New International Version

As a child, my experience of God was a feeling, a presence, a knowing. There was a sense that this world was not all that there was. It was so tangible, and the veil felt so thin that I remember praying as a child while playing in the basement family room, "Don't let me see anything, because that would scare me." I guess that ended any chance of seeing my guardian angel while here on this side.

God has spoken in a variety of ways and used others to reach me throughout the journey. I grew up under the care and blessing of very loving parents who introduced me to God and life navigation. On rides to school every day, my Dad imparted his practical wisdom, taught me the value of laughter as a life strategy, and helped me through the tough times with advice like, "Just because somebody says it doesn't make it true. If they're not talking about you yet, they'll get around to you. If they are, they'll soon move on to someone else." At the point of college decision-making, the brochure at a private women's Christian college fell open in my mother's hands to information about a full scholarship that would enable me to obtain an education that was otherwise unaffordable. When it was time for graduate school, something I had not really contemplated, it was the Dean who called me to his office with the announcement that I must apply for a scholarship that led to an international education. At the time, it seemed a fairy tale to dream of living in another country, and yet, it happened and was a door-opening experience later on. I was also protected from the recession that left many new graduates without job prospects. Clearly, God had a plan He was using to tee up my life and His expectations of me. Most definitely, He was using other people to guide me.

However, at some point, you have to graduate into a life in complete relationship to Him that requires more of you. You have to choose. While

I followed the path, gained skills that would be needed, and attempted to build a life, in hindsight, I realize for a time I stopped co-creating with God and ventured out on my own. God went quiet, even in my calling, as I toyed with a journey that was not of His making.

As a small child, I wanted to be a nun. This was not a profession of religious denomination but a feeling of connection, proximity, and a desire to be of service. It stems back to that "knowing." My passions were learning, history, archaeology, dance, reading, and travel combined with gifts of speaking and writing. I had no idea how to use these blessings or the qualities people saw in me to create a successful life or livelihood beyond academics. Frustrated, I felt like my life was on hold. I kept blasting ahead, not addressing the things that prevented Him from taking action with me in one respect, and in the other was paralyzed.

In that failure to co-create, I wandered in the desert for a few years. God always gives us the choice of whether we seek Him or not. Finally, after aimlessly bumbling around, I sought Him specifically. Frustrated, exasperated, tired, confused, and thirsty from the desert, I prayed from the depths of my soul, *"I'll go where you want and do what you want, even if it's not somewhere I think I want to go, if you'll just take my life and make something of it."*

The moment of surrender became the moment of transformation. God wasted no time when He got that text message from me. The next day, the phone rang with the job that gave my life direction, a career, and answered the childhood "knowing" of a life of service. Of course, it came through my mother, and of course, it was back in my hometown. By the way, He tested that obedience declaration periodically. There were assignments that came along that surely weren't in locations where my family or I wanted to be, nor were they filled with fields of clover and wildflowers all the time. I did remain obedient, though sometimes ungraciously protesting. However, this life of service has delivered more blessings, fabulous people and friendships, strength, and growth than I could have imagined or designed, even with the trials that have accompanied the journey.

In Romans 12:2, Paul reminds us, *"Do not conform to the pattern of this world, but be transformed by the renewing of your mind. Then, you will be able to test and approve what God's will is – His good, pleasing and perfect will."*[2]

In that moment of surrender, I chose Him, and He unveiled His will for my life plan by plan. Thereafter began the next phase of transforming a life into a calling. I had no idea that the threads of my life, through sin and pain, would become an opportunity to support and care for others professionally as an executive coach, spiritually as a Christian coach, to teach, write, speak, consult and travel the world. His will. His plan. His timing. He seeks us in the midst of our plans and our sin. Our choice is whether to be in relationship, obedience, and transformation.

We never know how many soul days we have here or when it's going to change or end on the earthly front porch. When the veil is removed, and we stand at The Throne, how do we want to answer whether our calendar was full of Him or not? When sudden illness or tragedy strikes our families, friends, colleagues – or us? Is that when we want our eyes to be opened?

This book is intended as a guide gift for your journey. I have shared stories of my personal life, both joyful and challenging, to help you reflect

---

[2] Romans 12:2, New International Version

on your story, to jog you into remembering your life's vignettes, and to encourage you to see the filaments that weave your journey together, bridging the Heavenly and earthly front porches. Each chapter gives you space to rest, think, and design the next phase with Him, tips to help you pursue new options, behaviors, and strategies, and prayers to help you connect porch to Porch. At the end, there is a summary and co-creation templates to which you can return throughout your life, revisit where you are, and continue designing with Him. No matter whether you are single or married, employed or unemployed, a new graduate, a newlywed, considering retirement, or looking for a career change; taking some time to visit and revisit your journey with Him is an investment that will give you the highest return on your life as you seek to fulfill your calling.

This book isn't meant to be devoured but is a workbook for your journey as you co-create a porch to Porch Plan. Read a chapter, do the work, connect to your stories, remember, listen, and come back as you move forward. Don't rush ahead and jump to other chapters. It's a process. If something doesn't resonate with you yet, don't worry about it. Listen for what speaks to you, and remember, you may be in the preparation space where God gets you ready for the next assignment. Let the words plant seeds for your future harvesting. Trust God's guidance and timing.

I hope that by doing some "Soul Sittin'" while on this earthly front porch that you will connect to the Heavenly Front Porch, search your heart, listen for His voice, design your life in partnership, and accept a transformed life by saying "Yes!" to His call. It happened for me, and with courage and grace, it is yours to accept.

***May your front porch always be full
and connected – porch to Porch!***

The author shortly after arrival on the earthly front porch

"Before I formed you in the womb, I knew you."[3]

HEAVEN'S FRONT PORCH

We awake each day into how we have defined now, whether intentionally or by default; born of decision heaped upon decision. We live what we have created, and we measure our success based on a system we have developed over time, whether we realize it or not. Some look at their bank accounts, investments, and real estate holdings. Others admire the clothes or jewelry they wear. The quality and quantity of cars or club and golf course memberships capture the attention of many. A few hold up their professional titles and the initials before or after their names. Others recall the number of places they have traveled. Some look at the size of their home or the number of their homes. Still

---

[3] Jeremiah 1:5, New International Version

others review their list of awards and public recognition, examine the frequency of their social media likes and mentions, and look to other external reinforcements. We are all seeking feedback on how we are doing. There is nothing wrong with any of the above in and of themselves as measurements of various forms of progress or accomplishment in our lives. However, collectively, they are focused primarily on external validation and "me" without the slightest mention of impacts on anyone else. Is it really all about me?

Are we missing the ultimate measure of a life well lived in synchrony with the intention for our presence on this earth? As we seek how to discern our progress, we forget our origins and that there are other considerations that refocus our "how much/how many" questions. Where did we use our influence to improve the conditions of others? How many trips did we take to see the standards of care that could be improved somewhere and give of our time to assist those in need? When did we sacrifice intended leisure time for someone who needed us? Did we notice at work what the real work was as opposed to a list of tasks? Where were we when someone needed us to listen? When did we decide what enough looked like? What did we give up so that someone else could be secure? When have we stepped outside our comfort zones without knowing where the answers, resources, or destiny were going to take us? Did we remember to whom the resources we have really belong? As stewards, what have we been entrusted with as investors on earth, and how are we serving those gifts, talents, and assets?

Prior to our arrival on earth, imagine the excitement as everyone gathers on Heaven's Front Porch to wish the new soul a safe journey. There is such chatter, joy, and energy. Love is as loud as the rustling of the angels' wings as all push onto Heaven's Front Porch for a better view of the departure. The guardian angel is in front poised to take flight for a new assignment. Family members from generations past clasp their hands in anticipation, knowing how precious the first breath will be the moment the earthly parents embrace their treasured bundle. The people on earth entrusted by God to watch over, nourish, care for, and develop another servant anxiously await the birthday. A heavenly and earthly community gathers above and below the clouds to celebrate the relationships that will be cherished in the years to come.

There is expectation of how we will be together coming from Heaven's Front Porch. The angels and ancients have been in relationship for millennia and know the beauty of community. The Heavenly Front Porch is now bursting with these well-wishers. The space is crowded with love; over-joyed with the new beginning, and they remember.

The ancients recall how, during their earthly journey, people showed up for each other. They brought food and left it on the porch when times were tough. They waved to each other as they went by their neighbors' front porches acknowledging the blessing that it was to have others on their journey. They returned borrowed items to the porch with thanks in their hearts. They had their first kisses standing under the porch lights. They sat together and shared dreams on the porch. They played music and created an atmosphere of celebration through their songs and music. Their children fumbled with toys and games amidst their bubbly play chatter. They prayed together for others and lifted their hearts in praise at the beauty of the flowers blooming at the edge of the porch. They raised their eyes beyond the porch roof at night and marveled at the beauty of stars winking at them from unfathomable distances. With hopes and dreams, they prayed for possibility with faith in an unseen God, whose evidence was visible in everything around their earthly front porch.

The expectations from those on the Heavenly Front Porch are that we open our eyes, clean out our ears, be from the heart, and yearn from the spirit for the Spirit. With these prayers in their hearts for us, they have all wished us well on our way as we each moved from the Heavenly Front Porch to the earthly front porch. Oh the hope, the dreams, the feelings that maybe this one will hear, see, know, and consistently yield to the connections with the Heavenly Front Porch throughout their life from the very beginning. They yearn to help bridge us to the heavenly Father through the stories of their own walks, their trials and failings, and their prayers for us from the ancient days until today.

Another burst of energy surges through the angels and ancients as the new soul is paraded towards the Heavenly Front Porch. The guardian angel is handed the precious cargo that will become a newborn in its final journey from Porch to porch. With prayers for a safe journey, the rustling stills as all fall to their knees in praise of creation's continued miracle from the heavenly Father.

There was a day when they all gathered on the Heavenly Front Porch for you and entrusted you for a time to the earthly front porch. What has happened for you so far after you journeyed from Porch to porch? What have you designed, and with whom have you created it? How will you charter the course for the next phase between the porches?

SOUL SITTIN': TRAVELING FROM THE HEAVENLY FRONT PORCH

1. As a child, what **expectations** did you have of your life that you have lost?

2. What would it take to **recapture** your dreams?

3. What is the earliest story you can remember of **feeling connected** to the Heavenly Front Porch?

4. What can you point to that demonstrates your **awareness** that your life is a gift?

5. How are you **honoring the miracle** of your life and your Creator?

6. What immediately springs to your mind and your gut that is **out of alignment** in your life? Personally? Professionally? Spiritually?

7. What do you believe the **purpose** of your life is up to this point?

8. What would the world be like **if you had not been born**? What would be missing? Who would be missing? What work would have gone undone?

9. Do you see your **purpose morphing** in any way in the future? What **evidence** can you point to for your assessment?

10. What are you **willing** to do to realign yourself with the Heavenly Front Porch expectations for your life?

11. If you choose not to fully step into your purpose for the rest of your life, what is likely to be left **undone** that could affect other people and their quality of life? What might you miss out on?

12. When are you willing to **begin**?

13. **Who** are you willing to tell that you are beginning?

SOUL SITTIN' TIPS:

1. Contact relatives who remember you from childhood. Ask them to describe you as they remember you throughout your development and to share the stories of your journey. Listen for the characteristics of your personality, the natural preferences for how you used your time, your favorite toys, and the roles that you took in play. Look for the threads in others' stories that give clues to who you were in the early arrival years. We often forget whom we are and become covered in layers of who we have become while on life's journey. Step one is finding you again.

2. Step two is remembering your own stories. Grab your iPad, laptop, or a journal and start capturing the moments that you remember that were formative in your life, good and bad. What you may perceive as formative may not align with what others recollect. However, recognizing the scope of influences in your life is helpful in uncovering who you have become versus who you are meant to be.

If you are comfortable that you are where you are intended to be, neither of these exercises may ring true to you. Feel free to move beyond, but test yourself first to ensure that you are not avoiding something that may be uncomfortable to pursue. Trust yourself to take these steps to begin your journey.

For those who are feeling uncomfortable just reading these first two tips, there is probably work to be done in this area. Take some solace in the blessing below as you begin.

SOUL SITTIN' BLESSING FOR THE JOURNEY

"Ask, and it will be given to you; seek, and you will find; knock, and the door will be opened to you."[4]

I'm just starting out and feeling unsure about this journey that I'm undertaking. I don't completely understand the earthly and Heavenly Front Porches yet, but I know that something requires my attention. I feel the need to put the time in to explore what I might uncover, how I might be able to connect to my own stories, and identify whether there is a calling that I have yet to fully answer. I ask for strength so that I can maintain my resolve to read and participate in this fully, for courage to dissect where I might be and what I might need to adjust in the future, and for openness to the messages for me. Help me to connect to the Heavenly Front Porch each time I sit down with this book and to recognize in its pages the reasons You have for me to be using this tool on my journey. As my awareness increases, plant in me a desire to continue for the whole trip.

---

[4] Matthew 7:7, New International Version

Spraker family farm with kind permission of the author's cousin: Susan Spraker

"Who am I, Lord God, and what is my family,
that you have brought me this far?" [5]

FRONT PORCH HOMECOMINGS

To get to my grandparents' farm in Southwest, Virginia, otherwise known as "The Homestead founded in 1912," turn off the interstate and lollygag through a small main street where the local office supply store peels your attention away with a pencil of outrageous proportions dangling off the front of the building.

---

[5] 1 Chronicles 17: 16, New International Version

With kind permission of Karen Gates, agoodsnapshot.blogspot.com

Tootle along the state road for a while and meander out into a rolling countryside of farms, mobile homes, barns, and utility buildings. Swing right, and head back up the hill by a long since passed on Great Uncle's home, and keep on going back into the hills. Turn left off that road to a narrower country road, passing farmhouses with mailboxes leaning so close to the road they threaten to divide your mirrors into tiny glass diamonds. Another right turn off that road onto the gravel road recalls the time a relative visiting from England for the first time said, "Where ARE you taking me?" Still one more left turn just before Aunt Ola's house takes you into the country lane that winds past the springhouse and over several cattle guards that require getting out to open and close gates – a high point on the three-hour journey when I was a child.

Just before the last bend to the left in the lane, the fold in the road allows you to glimpse the site of the white farmhouse with the big front porch. It sits way back in the holler past the barn and the out buildings where the cistern joins them from a time gone by. It was at that moment when excitement peaked, because they were almost always waiting there on the front porch. Grandma would be in a chair next to the swing on one side of the door and Granddad in a chair on the other side next to the glider. There was never such a plummeting of your stomach if for some reason one of them wasn't on the porch waiting, because the next moment of homecoming was always especially sweet.

Author's Grandparents: Stephen & Cynthia Spraker

Out of the car we would rush, through the two boxwood guardians at the fence gate. Flying to the front porch, arms waited to enfold you in love and time made precious by distance's theft. My grandmother's ample "shelf," as she called it, was a place of comfort, rest, peace, and unconditional love. My Grandfather's cigar fragranced shirts and the smile on his face could never be replaced with a starched shirt smelling of "spring freshness." With eyes closed, I am the child again in these magical visits. Hanging in my home today is a tapestry of a white front porch surrounded by nearby flowers and pillow-plumped havens to settle into, because it reminds me of experiencing what matters.

It was the front porch where the center of activity occurred when the three brothers brought their families together to visit. My eldest cousin, Steve, would sit on the swing and play the banjo as background for all the catching up of the six first cousins. There was a "Spraker way" of humor, laughter, jokes, and story telling that the men kept alive and passed on to their sons. You never felt more yourself or more at home than in this setting.

It was on that front porch that I learned about shucking corn and shelling peas, repairing one's finger from an angry corn worm, that work could be social, and it also has a sting at times. It was here that we returned with lightening bugs in a jar at dusk, and I began to live up to being my Grandmother's namesake as a "Bringer of light." Standing on that same front porch, my Grandmother laughed with her whole body at my cousin and I when we left our huckleberry picking results in an open plastic container in a stump over night. Of course, we intended to return the next day to continue our berry gathering, expecting that they would still be there amidst the hungry wildlife. Herein lies an early example of survival wisdom being passed from generation to generation on the earthly front porch or maybe awakening just plain old common sense.

That front porch was witness to my cousins prancing around the yard with sparklers, competing with the twilight sky. It felt the hard landing as I raced back to safety after being rescued from the pigpen and a very inhospitable sow. Standing on that porch, I watched my border collie round up the sheep away from where they were meant to be for shearing and observed a very unhappy father engaging in unexpected shepherding. Life lessons abounded on what can be created when one goes astray from one's purpose.

It was while we gathered around on that porch that my Grandfather passed on the family history as we listened to one yarn after another of stories about "our people." It was on the porch that the sound of my Grandmother's voice singing hymns, or occasionally "Cripple Creek," drifted out from the kitchen. As those tunes were absorbed into your very fiber, the knowledge permeated that while she was with us, she was very aware of her ultimate journey towards the other Porch. The gift of knowing where you've come from carries you through the decades as you find out and refine who you are, tying the generations together with fine filaments that hold you steady when you move up a rung on the ladder of life. As my dear mentor, Dr. Billy Wireman once told me, "Never forget where you come from."

Oral story telling's art has been a home for sharing the experience of life through the millennia. The magic of the front porch and homecomings were about "being" together, relating, sharing, laughing, teasing, and loving. It was about time. Time spent with each other. Time invested in each other. Time gone that no one can take back from any of us.

You see the grandparents are long gone to the Heavenly Front Porch joining the angels and the ancients. One of the three brothers is gone. One of the cousins is gone. One of the aunts is gone, but the front porch homecomings still remain. They live on in the tapestry in our house. They live on in the knowledge of who we are and where we originated. They live on in the stories we now tell. They live on in our memories.

It was the experiences during the homecomings that made them magical when we were together. It wasn't what any of us did for a living. It wasn't what any of us wore that day. It wasn't what we drove to get there. It was that we were there, present in each other's lives while we were on the earthly front porch.

SOUL SITTIN': CREATING A LIFE OF FRONT PORCH HOMECOMINGS

1. What are the sounds, smells, stories, and memories that **evoke your ties** to the earthly front porch?

2. Who was present for you then – a teacher, friend's parent, grandparents, siblings, parents, pastor, sports coach, bus driver, or a Sunday school teacher? Who were your **shepherds**?

3. What do you miss from your childhood that you could **replicate** to keep those experiences, impressions, and groundings alive?

4. What are you doing now to **create a homecoming front porch experience** for your immediate family that will be their treasured memories and foundation for the future?

5. Is your **family more important** than work, soccer practice, cleaning house, or your virtual life?

6. What are you willing to give up to **be**, share, and enjoy together?

7. What have you done lately to let the people you love know you are **present** for and with them?

8. If someone in your immediate family died next week, what **regrets** would you have about the quality of the relationships that you have created with them on your family's front porch?

9. What memories reinforce your **connection to the Heavenly Front Porch** as a child? Even if you think you have always been disconnected, go deeper and think about walks in the woods, bicycle rides, playing on your own, reading a story at night, sitting on the beach, or feeling sad or lonely. When were there whispers from the Heavenly Front Porch even if you didn't have the language to express it?

SOUL SITTIN' TIPS:

1. **Prioritize** your family on your calendar. Make at least a weekly appointment with each other.

2. **Recognize** that every day gone is a day lost. It's about your experiences together, not whether you have the latest gadget, car, or the biggest house.

3. **Show up.** Put down the iPad, smart phone, book, and vacuum cleaner, and be present. Being in the same room, at the dinner table, or in the car together is not being there for each other. Pay attention. Listen with intention and look them in the eye. Acknowledge each other.

4. **Create** a video library of your family's oral history. Bridge the generations by collecting the long ago stories from the patriarchs and matriarchs of your family and add recent family tales from your kids and grandkids.

   a. Engage the tech savvy kids with smartphone and camcorder videos.
   b. Start a family YouTube channel.
   c. Play a selection at the next family reunion.
   d. Keep it growing with all the special events as your family grows.

5. **Preserve** your family in your blog or post them on throwback Thursday to your Facebook page. Keep them close to your heart.

6. Pick one of the above and **START** this week.

SOUL SITTIN' BLESSING FOR ARRIVALS

"Quick! Bring the best robe and put it on him.
Put a ring on his finger and sandals on his
feet... Let's have a feast and celebrate."[6]

God of relationships, one family, and prodigals; help me to know that I have a homecoming awaiting me. Let me feel that the front porch is full of those excited about my return, just as they were filled with anticipation when I arrived here. No matter how far away I have strayed from the Porch, let me know You are there waiting for me with arms outstretched, a chair with my name on it, music to soothe my soul, and refreshment.

Let me also be a creator of homecomings for others and a source of memories that evoke the best of a life well-lived porch to Porch. If there is work I need to do here to mend my earthly relationships, help me to have the courage to do that, to clean up my own front porch so that those whom I've loved and who loved me can find a homecoming waiting for them. If I need to return to a front porch first and hold out my arms, help me to go and to keep it simple. When my family reaches out to me, help me to behave in a way that lets them know they are my priority and to let go of those things that get in the way of me being a homecoming for them. When they arrive before me, let me treat them, as I know You will treat me, when I arrive for the greatest Homecoming of all.

---

[6] Luke 15: 22-23, New International Version

"My Presence will go with you, and I will give you rest." [7]

THE EMPTY FRONT PORCH:
BUSY, TIRED, DEAF US

Have you noticed your neighborhood lately? Front porches abound in older and newer neighborhoods with big columns in the Antebellum style, Victorian round towers with their graceful connected porches, Louisiana grillwork porches and balconies, wrap-arounds and L's, concrete bases with grill lacework slats across ranches, and cabins with their log hat entrances. Year after year, *Southern Living* magazine's covers highlight front porches filled with afternoon teas and delectable goodies all laid out in spring, summer, and fall splendor tempting us to an era when we made time to decorate, create, and stop. Take a look at the newer apartment and condo buildings. First floor levels have

---

[7] Exodus 33:14, New International Version

patios out back in memory of the front porch but are locked away from communal interaction. Higher floors have small balconies reminiscent of the front porch but still create separation. Our porches and patios are usually beautifully decorated with statuettes, flowers, wicker garden furniture, brightly colored pillows, and inviting spaces.

And they're empty.

Our magazine covers, photos, and decorating attempts seem to draw us towards a time when what it meant to have a front porch was to be with family and to enjoy neighbors who could drop by without notice. There was time for eating snacks together in the humid summer afternoon, meeting up with friends for a good ole chat, curling up in the swing and reading a good book, watching the kids playing in the yard or running through the sprinkler, or watering beautiful pots of ferns and hanging baskets. It screams of time to simply be human beings as a necessary part of our experience in living a quality life. Not idle boring time. Not being pulled by any number of to do lists. Not being controlled by content flowing at us like we are automatons directly connected to our inboxes. As Miranda Lambert's 2014 hit "Automatic" so eloquently yearns, "It all just seemed so good the way we had it, back before everything became automatic."[8] Those of us who can remember clamor in our hearts for the way back and feel real concern for our children for whom we have not provided these experiences. We wonder how we can pass on what this means before it's too late.

---

[8] Lambert, Hemby, Galyon Lyrics, "Automatic," *Platinum* (RCA Nashville, 2014) http://www.en.m.wikipedia.org.

Technology has given us the ability to solve problems more quickly, to share our solutions globally in a split second, and to understand cultures and world events more thoroughly. The access to knowledge is rapidly working towards both improving and decimating human society at the same time. We are so exhausted from the race and the racket that the sale of noise cancelling earphones has gone through the roof![9] On the one hand, we are delivering more noise more effectively through earbuds. On the other hand, we are cancelling each other out.

As we are forced to adjust to the speed of information hurling at us, enhance our discernment ability, and evolve at the most rapid pace ever known to humans, we are depleted. We have inadvertently joined a race that has created consequences individually and for our communities. Without regular attention to them, they steal our lives, the quality of our lives, and our spirits. This state of being calls for awareness and discipline, so the positive results of our gains won't be wiped out by the negative impacts.

We are so busy and time deficient now that we have to schedule time just to be, providing we even realize we need to do so, and then fight feeling guilty. Many of my coaching clients come to me from a place of deprivation, though those are not the words that are used to define why they want to enter into a coaching relationship. It is framed in, "I need a new job." "I've got to get out of here." "I don't know how to handle what is being expected of me." "I have to work on my work/life balance." "I'm stuck." "I don't know what I want, but this is not it." "I could use

---

[9] "Premium Headphone Sales Account for Over 90% of Headphone Revenue growth in Q1, 2013, according to the NPD Group." "March 2012 – March 2013, noise cancelling as a feature increased from 49% to 55%." Port Washington, NY, June 5, 2013 http://www.npd.com.

another perspective on my life and my career." And it's across all ages. At a church retreat, a woman contributed that she once heard that the definition of busy is "being under Satan's yoke."[10] Busy drains our focus away from the most important beings who should fill our front porch and with whom we are yoked in this life – God, family, and friends.

What we are feeling, and in many cases are unable to label, is an empty spirit. Think about the last time that you purchased gas. Not only are there the noises of your own car, the traffic, sirens from emergency vehicles, and the surge of fluid as you pump; but the gas station blasts music into the outdoors just to be sure that pumping gas is a pleasurable experience for you. It's gas! It takes less than five minutes, but how on earth can we go without some content being pushed to us to fill the void of empty space? That's the very space where creation happens. It's the space where you can hear your voice, your dreams, your desires, your internal warning system, and the voice of God. That's where the Porch intersects with the porch and where you fill up your spirit.

In the times in which we live, we have bought into an inaccuracy that twelve hour days are giving our employers our best, what they are due, and what is necessary for the U.S. to be competitive, along with a sense of security that we will remain employed. We now have a nation of sleep deprived people, who are essentially the equivalent of being drunk at work in terms of how our brain capacity functions. The CDC has declared "insufficient sleep a public health epidemic" after conducting a Behavioral Risk Factor Surveillance System survey, which

---

[10] "B.U.S.Y." Mike Riley, Montana Street Church of Christ, El Paso, TX, 5/24/00 http://www.theseeker.org.

noted that 38% of respondents fell asleep once in the previous month,[11] presumably not at bedtime. It endangers people's lives from the safety of our commute to our safety at work. We have the option to alter our current model by choosing to live a full front porch life, filling up our spirits, our physical beings, and our lives.

Years ago when I was in a job transition, I conducted an experiment. I was exhausted from the preparation of a significant move, getting a house ready to sell, determining what was going to go with us, finding a new home, wrapping up a treasured job, taking care of the people I was leaving behind, unpacking, and getting settled in a new community. I decided to take two months between jobs to tackle the second part of the move gradually, to learn my new community, to enjoy time with my husband, and to get rested before what are always steep learning and performance curves the first year of a new leadership position. In addition, I created some space for myself during this sabbatical to not have to do. Stepping off of life's treadmill provided time for insights and perspective that can get lost as we rush from moment to moment.

To do this, I completely disconnected from the world with two exceptions, providing our immediate family and my successor our contact information in case of emergency. I posted nothing on LinkedIn about a change in position, created no postings on Facebook, and staggeringly, I did not engage in email much. For two months, it was almost like the days of someone having to phone or write to be in touch. All of a sudden, there was life space.

---

[11] "Insufficient Sleep is a Public Health Epidemic," January 13, 2014, http://www. CDC.gov/features/dsleep.

The experiment yielded a number of interesting results. The first was a greater sense of peace in our lives. Instead of living to others' expectations, we were taking charge of how we spent our time together, putting our family first, and also caring for the new people who would come into our lives by preparing ourselves with some much needed rejuvenation. What we learned was that given the significance of the changes, we had actually under-estimated how much time we needed. A third month would have been ideal.

The second observation was how unhappy people were at our unannounced absence. It's always nice to have people want your presence in their lives. Yet this had a feeling of control to it, as if we did not have the right to design our lives, determine the immediate needs we had, act on them, and focus time on family. It was almost as if the message was, "Because I'm choosing to remain trapped inside this environment, how dare you point out that there is an alternative option to exercise." Our choice led to self-examination by some and surfaced some unexpected reflection for others. A number expressed a wish that they had the luxury of that same time. For anyone we scared by our absence, we sincerely apologized. Admittedly, life circumstances can restrict the ability to step away in the same manner that we did. However, we had designed our lives to provide this as a choice.

The third thing we noticed was that we were spending less time on the Internet and with TV and more time interacting. After decades of handling schedules of national and international travel, so much of our time when we were together was taking care of what had to be dealt with before the next excursion. The self-limitation of reducing distractions was giving us back the quality in our life.

This is not a commentary on the use of the Internet, its value as a tool, the extraordinary way in which it allows us to stay in contact with people, or the benefits of global collaboration to solve the world's challenges. It is nothing other than an observation that with the volume of options that we have today, we have a new responsibility to discern and make decisions about how we use the most valuable resource we will ever have - our time on this earth. We can either remain detached, distracted, and devoid of meaningful connection, or we can connect porch to Porch eliminating the empty spirit syndrome.

SOUL SITTIN': FILLING UP YOUR FRONT PORCH

How you fill up the front porch of your life impacts the quality of every day and the state of your spirit. Give some consideration to:

1. If you have one now at your home, describe **your physical front porch**, patio, screened-in porch, balcony, or back deck as it exists now.

   a. What uses do you, your family, and friends make of this area?
   b. How would you like that to change?
   c. What would you physically add to this space to prepare it appropriately?
   d. What agreements do you need to make with others to embrace this area of your home, and how you would like them to connect to your porch?

2. On a scale of 1-5, with 5 being the most full, where would you describe the **state of your spirit** at the moment?

3. If you were offered 35 hours per week, or 5 hours per day, of your life back, is how you are living now, **how you would choose to spend it**? If not, what changes would you make? Add your alterations to your "Soul Sittin' Vision: porch to Porch Plan". (Appendix A.)

4. Where are you placing **inappropriate priority** to your emails, Instagram, Twitter, Facebook, the TV, on-line gaming, etc.?

5. What opportunities are you missing for God to show up in your life, or for you to show up in someone else's life, by the **behaviors you engage in that are drowning out your life**?

6. Where in your life can you **reclaim time**?

7. Where are you allowing others, besides God, to **direct your life**?

8. How often is the **Creator on your calendar**? Is it a mindless time to go to church once a week, or do you have time set aside each day to be with God? Is it a quick, "Lord, could you take care of this," or is it waiting and listening from Samuel's spirit of "Here I am?"[12] How empty has Jesus' calendar been on a daily basis?

---

[12] 1 Samuel 3:4, New International Version

SOUL SITTIN' TIPS:

1. Consider limiting your TV viewing, Internet, and social media interactions. When engaging in these activities, evaluate the enrichment they are providing to your life and the contribution they make to a full spirit.

2. Maximize every option that your email system has that will minimize the daily onslaught, including changing your settings so it doesn't flash on your screen every time an email comes through. Use *unsubscribe* liberally, and reduce the influx into your inbox.

3. Take out your earbuds and consider the conversations that might happen in the grocery store, on the plane, and at work if you weren't so sure that the content that was being pushed to you was more important than the potential interactions with other spirits. Yes, we are "spiritual beings having a human experience,"[13] who are blocking our channels to each other and God. Next

---

[13] Pierre Teilhard de Chardin, http://www.brainyquote.com.

week, count how many times you have an interaction with a new person and note it to yourself. Work on increasing this exponentially in the months to come.

4. Schedule a mini-sabbatical. You may not be able to take months away from your life, but everyone can find a day or a half day a month that can be your sabbatical from email, TV, internet, and your to do list. Schedule YOU on your calendar starting next month.

5. Give yourself permission to design your life in a way that is free from others' expectations of you. This is not about neglecting your children, spouse, elderly parents, or your job. This is about learning to say, "No" to the things that we allow others to manipulate us into. What can you let go of today?

6. Consider taking morning prayer walks that provide the space to step away from the daily pressures of life. They allow you to get your mind, body, and spirit in shape at the same time, while creating a discipline around how you order your priorities. Recognize that as you walk, pray, and think, you will wander between sitting on the Porch and stepping off on your own. You may have to keep pulling yourself back from life's lists as you practice preventing this from being something else to check off.

7. Adjust your schedule to start your day sitting on the Heavenly Front Porch. The rest of your day will go much better and sometimes in directions that bear no resemblance to your calendar, because you went to His Front Porch for a visit first.

SOUL SITTIN' BLESSING FOR PRIORITIES AND SERENITY

"For where your treasure is, there your heart will be also."[14]

I'm busy, tired, deaf, and empty. I crave space, quiet, and peace. Right now, I don't know where to start to co-create a future. My to do lists are books, and I have a shelf full of them between work, family, church, and volunteer obligations. Sometimes, I have one that is so big that the others aren't even on my radar. I'm so intense that I've forgotten there are other parts of my life that should be receiving my focus.

Help me to shut out the noise so I can revisit and reestablish the real priorities for my life. I don't want to be deaf to You, and yet, I don't seem to be able to stop. I want off the treadmill so that I can begin to live authentically, purposefully, intentionally, and reasonably. Help me create space on my calendar for the things that You want in my life, including You. Give me the courage to let go of bad habits that steal my precious time, the one resource that is finite on the earthly front porch. In the creation of new space, help me to settle into the feeling of peace, and keep me from rushing to clog the spaces back up as You fill up my empty spirit instead.

---

[14] Luke 12:34, New International Version

"Be Still and Know that I am God."[15]

FRONT PORCH BYPASSES

When our grandson was about three years old, we went to England for a family visit. This was the first time he might remember us later. When we came into the house, his little voice said, "Are you my Granddad from America?" When my husband responded that he was, in broad Yorkshire, the little tyke said, "Come in. Sit down. Have a cup of tea!"

At three years old, my grandson had nailed exactly what it means to be hospitable. Come *be* with us in spirit. Come rest *with* us in company. Let us take *care* of you by providing your body with refreshment. *Be with*

[15] Psalm 46:10, New International Version

care. While more than twenty years later, we still laugh heartily at our encounter with his well-worded invitation, we noted he had already been taught inside the family circle the priorities of being, being together, and taking care of one another.

While the home did not have a physical front porch, through his invitations, he created a front porch. Through his presence, his words, and his commitment to us, he declared his intentions for us. He did not allow us the option of driving right on by the front porch and missing the opportunities that hanging out together could bring and the memories we would create together. Imagine how we felt after flying three thousand miles to be welcomed in this way to our homecoming.

This was before cell phones, laptops, and the Internet, when fast living was going through a drive-through. This was when relationships were still relational and not transactional; when from whom you bought your car was your neighbor in town who had worked hard to get the dealership brought to your area. In this era, your dentist was the father of one of your classmates, and you saw both of them on field trips. Your insurance agent was the guy who sat a few pews up from you in church. People knew that the real work of life cannot be done at speed.

I remember vividly the day when I had a particularly long task list at work, how a transformational moment removed my bypass behavior and altered my understanding of my daily focus on this earth. I was playing the CEO role supporting people, moving strategy forward, juggling resources, and wondering how on earth I was going to accomplish what needed attention that day. For some reason, I connected that morning in a different way with God. At this point in my life, I considered my work to be my form of ministry and tried to represent my faith consistently.

However, it dawned on me that I was just living life by a task list. That day, I prayed before I left home, "Show me the real work."

I dutifully started peddling through my insanely long "to do's," and suddenly a staff member appeared at my office door absolutely distraught. I stopped answering email, moved out from behind the barrier of my desk to sit with the person, and gave my full attention. As the personal challenges were unloaded, I realized, "Ahhh...this is the real work for today." To be perfectly honest, while I knew this was what I was supposed to be focusing on, there was a little bit of tension that remained in me regarding that list. I pushed away the head nagging and continued focusing on the person in distress. By the end of the day, the staff member was calm, and the ancillary items I had considered so important were completed, minus the anticipated stress. I was astonished. That life breakthrough brought the realization that no matter what I was engaged in, my life is given in service to the Porch. I have an amazing Boss who takes care of everything.

The "ah ha" of realizing that I was living my life by a task list still needed further attention. While there is no denying that there is the stuff of life that has to be handled, there are very few deadlines that cannot be dealt with in a way that is different from "the world is going to come to an end." Paying the mortgage, making the IRS tax deadline, and getting the kids to school on time, I'll give you those. However, if we died now, much of what is on life's task list isn't going to get done, and frankly, isn't going to matter.

What does matter is when your wife says, "Could we just sit and talk for a while?" or your husband says, "Honey, can I take you out to breakfast?" What does matter is when someone on your team needs you, and it's not for the project you're both working on. What does matter is that you honor the primary relationships in your life. "Honor your father and your mother"[16] didn't have a caveat of "when you feel like it" or only if they have given me "x" in life or after I watch my favorite TV program. It's not just a guide on how to live, it's a recognition that relational interactions are more important than transactional interactions, which are what we spend way too much of our lives doing.

We drive right on by the front porch in this mobile life of ours, take front porch bypasses, and think that we don't pay a price for it. We believe if we have texted twenty times a day that we have a relationship. We post on Facebook and Instagram and tweet content to worldwide audiences moment by moment, living our lives by over-communicating and under-relating to our great peril. The great distractor is stealing the richness of life and keeping us on over-drive trying to absorb it all, observe it all, contribute to it all, and yet for what? We need to stop living our lives as one big long list to be checked off and start thinking about whom we should be focusing our time and attention upon.

I had the distinct privilege of being part of a business group called C12 for a year. The members were committed to lead their businesses as a form of ministry. One of the member benefits is a built-in council of advisors. During a particularly busy time in my professional life, I made a presentation about my company, The Leaders' Haven. I was seeking their wisdom on how to make some decisions about my life, my multiple leadership roles, and the continuing growth of my company. One of my friends in the group, Todd Rhodes, said, "Slow down to speed up." I

---

[16] Exodus 20:12, New International Version

gnawed on this counsel, felt very conflicted about stepping back, and pondered how to go about doing this.

What came to light was that while I felt like I was firing on all cylinders, I was really burning out and was operating in too many directions at a pace that was unsustainable. I had taken away the space that allowed me to hear God's voice, my own voice, and those around me. I was so busy doing and accomplishing for people that I was not leaving enough time to be with people. The trade off of relational for transactional relationships has a very high price, the steepness of which is sometimes not realized until later when it is too late. I began activating an amazing two-letter word as I created space in my life by slowing down to speed up, "No."

SOUL SITTIN': SLOWING DOWN TO SPEED UP

As you continue to create your full front porch, address the following:

1. How, when, and how often am I **inviting others** onto my front porch?

2. What relationships am I bypassing by **treating them as transactions** that are making me poor in life and cheating them from a full front porch life with me? Make a list of areas that need improvement, and next to it, write what you are going to practice to change your behaviors.

3. When was the last time you asked to be shown the **real work of your life**? What do you know it to be now?

4. Where, and with whom, am I **over-communicating and under-relating**? Is it with:

   a. My children?
   b. My spouse?
   c. My boss?
   d. My staff/employees?
   e. My parents?
   f. My friends?

   How will I alter this behavior? What will others see as a result of this change?

5. How can I **slow down to speed up**?

6. Am I flying past God's front porch? If so, what do I need to do to **drive the heavenly speed limit** again?

7. To whom, or to what, do I need to start **saying, "No"**? What obligations can I reduce or eliminate and allow someone else to step into?

8. To what changes am I **willing to commit**: tomorrow, next week, or next month? Are they permanent changes?

SOUL SITTIN' TIPS:

1. Write down specifically where you are running too hard and too
    fast bypassing the earthly and Heavenly Front Porches.

    a. How is the current behavior affecting your life?
    b. What are you losing out on?
    c. Why are you perpetuating it?
    d. In your mind, what do you have to give up to stop?
    e. What are you putting at risk by continuing in this fashion?
    f. What are you willing to change?

2. Take a look at your calendar for the month and locate where the
    Heavenly Front Porch is intersecting with yours. Don't take the
    checklist approach of showed up, gave money, and sent a card
    to a sick friend. Where is your purposeful time to connect in a
    relational way and not a transactional one with your Creator?

SOUL SITTIN' BLESSING FOR PACE

"Come to me, all you who are weary and burdened, and I will give you rest."[17]

Install some tolls next to my front porch, so I will slow down and think twice about bypassing the Heavenly Front Porch. The things of this world are so attractive. The measurements of this world are so magnetic. The force field that these pressures create in my life leaves me feeling like I can't stop. I'm unable to even see at the moment where my interactions are more transactional than relational, because that is how my state of being has been for so long. Take off my blinders and help me to have panoramic vision.

I have a nagging feeling that I may also be over-communicating and under-relating. Let me check my accounts to see where I may have been telling my high school friends that I've picked up my dry cleaning or am on my way to buy groceries. I never called them on the phone to tell them these things, so why would they find them interesting now? I just might need an ego check and to pivot away from "Watch me! Watch me!" to "Watch Him! Watch Him!" If it's all about me, then how can it be about others and service? Help me to recognize that the marvelous tools of the time I live in are still best used to disseminate truth and help me get more work done for You.

---

[17] Matthew: 11: 28, New International Version

Give me the gift of your pace for my life and my peace with that. Help me to remember that everything in Your time is the right time. Keep me from using the doing as a block for the real work of my life, and prevent the great distractor from succeeding in encouraging a life of over-drive and under-achievement for You. "Slow me down, Lord."

SLOW ME DOWN, LORD

Slow me down, Lord.
Ease the pounding of my heart by the quieting of my mind.
Steady my hurried pace.
Give me, amidst the day's confusion
the calmness of the everlasting hills.

Break the tension of my nerves and muscles
with the soothing music of singing streams
that live in my memory.

Help me to know the magical, restoring power of sleep
Teach me the art
of taking minute vacations…
slowing down to look at a flower,
to chat with a friend,
to read a few lines from a good book.

Remind me
of the fable of the hare and the tortoise;
that the race is not always to the swift;
that there is more to life than measuring its speed.

Let me look up at the branches of the towering oak
and know that....it grew slowly....and well.

Inspire me
to send my own roots down deep...
into the soil of life's endearing values...

That I may grow toward the starts of my greater destiny.

Slow me down, Lord.[18]- Wilferd Arlan Peterson

---

[18] Slow me Down, Lord, Wilferd Arlan Peterson. Reprinted by kind permission of author's representative, Heacock Literary Agency, Inc., Cloudcroft, NM, USA.

"You will be secure because there is hope; you will look about you and take your rest in safety."[19]

THE DILAPIDATED FRONT PORCH

Sometimes we answer a calling and get so involved in it that we can no longer see if that is where we are still meant to be. We have vigorously prepared, rushed at it, shown up, thrown all of our talent at it, allowed ourselves to be consumed by it, and yet everything around us is getting cluttered up. There seems to be no time for any of the things that involve fulfilled relationships or maintenance of life. The clothes may be washed, but they're in piles everywhere. The car may run, but it hasn't been cleaned out in two years. The outdoor furniture may be on the porch, but the cover has been left off, and mildew has slimed everything. We get up with our families and go through the

---

[19] Job 11:18, New International Version

motions, but we're not connecting. We speak the words of love and care and get everyone where they should be all in the name of looking after them and going to work for God. We don't sit on the front porch anymore though.

As we've jogged through the weeks, we have moved into action without reflection. We have accelerated our doing, while the being that gives us focus and our center has drifted to the fog of a morning dream we can't quite grasp in context anymore. We keep telling ourselves it's all OK, because we're where we're supposed to be, and it's just the hard work we've been asked to do. In the end, we are developing shin splints from sprinting every second instead of training for the marathon with God. We're so busy doing "His work" that we run right by His Front Porch and don't even nod in recognition; so sure are we that we are on the right pace and know the track's layout. Our porch has become the cliché of a junked up mess with the washing machine out of place outside. The threat of falling through the hole at the top step creates a land mine, and if we lean on the railing, we'll pitch over backwards into the overgrown shrubs.

When our front porch has weeds poking through the wood slats, and we have to fight our way to the door through the mess, clinging to what we're doing even tighter becomes the reflexive response as selective blindness sets in. The justification is that I'm doing His work so everything else doesn't matter. In the midst of junking up our porch, we become vulnerable to inaccurate rationalizations for what we are doing, why we are doing it, and why we must continue in the same vein. We risk our partnership no longer being a co-creation with God. In a dilapidated front porch period in my life, a friend counseled, "Simplify." It was a way of saying, "Go to The Source and move away from complications.

Don't invite them into your life. Don't open the door off your front porch even a crack."

Another way of looking at the dilapidated front porch is through the lens of pride. When it becomes all about me, my service, my way of doing things, we sometimes cover the pride of what we are doing by saying we're doing it all for Him. Meanwhile our porch gets junked up with things that don't even remotely bear a resemblance to His work. We fill up our front porch with external validation that is not in conflict with our calling but that feeds our ego. We humbly collect our donor recognition for our personal gift or our outstanding award of service to "x." We say, "Yes" to the next project, because in the end, it's really about having the community see me succeed, yet again, because this is in my wheelhouse. What would we say to the next calling if it was all done anonymously and no plaques went up on our front porch as badges of our service?

To de-clutter our front porch first requires an acknowledgement that we have put the washing machine out there for all to see, and something frankly is out of place. We have to admit that we're not sure where to start on the project of cleaning it up and that the calling we've answered may have seen its time, or it may have turned into something that we've made all about us.

Step two requires going to The Source. Once we've had the "ah ha" and made the decision to go in search, we may find ourselves thwarted. It may come in the form of an inconvenience that messes up the timing of our plans. It may come in temptation to avoid the time blocked to connect. It may include an inconvenience like a job loss or lack of spousal support. The more we work to connect to the Heavenly Front

Porch, the more the distractor gets to work, and the more interruptions come our way to try to prevent success. It's why the daily discipline of seeking is essential to weaving the connective filament into a strong, knotted rope. It's our smartest move to prevent dilapidation from setting in.

I once entered a phase of life when I sensed that I was going to go through a particularly challenging desert walk. During that time, I attempted to stay connected and to take care of myself, which proved difficult to maintain. Knowing that there was a time when I would pull out of it, I established new boundaries in advance to prepare for altering my behavior when the time came and to set a line that I could see for how long I would allow my front porch to remain in a partially dilapidated state. It included rebalancing time commitments, re-establishing healthy exercise practices, putting God and my family in the appropriate priority, and getting consistent sleep.

While I was going through this period, my church announced a mountain retreat. It was to be at a location that has the look of the lodges I loved from my childhood riding the Virginia Blue Ridge Parkway and Skyline Drive and the peace of God's creation around it. The theme of the retreat was "Be Still." Given my state of depletion, I knew I was meant to be there.

About the same time, I came across a magazine article about a couple that had been called to build a chapel in the mountains in a different state from where they lived. They had no resources, no knowledge of where or why, and stepped out on faith obedient to the calling. I felt drawn to this chapel, and once I learned it was within range of the retreat, I decided to combine a visit on the same trip. Sometimes as one's porch is becoming dilapidated, preparation for the repairs and the next coat of paint are already in the works. I knew that I needed some maintenance, but I also had a lot of questions about where the next phase was headed. What I was completely unclear about was whether I was holding onto a calling from decades ago or whether my charge was to release the security and step out on faith in a new direction.

The drive to the chapel started on a Friday morning, with plenty of time and flexibility built in for quiet reflection there, before arriving at the retreat for the evening's first session. The article had warned not to use a GPS so I checked for directions on the website. Having grown up in the Shenandoah Valley with years spent in the surrounding mountains, I had no fear heading off on my own with my trusty all-wheel drive vehicle. I soon learned that when one is called into the wilderness alone for a meeting, the commitment to the journey can be as much of a test and preparation for getting your front porch back in shape as the chat itself.

Heading off, I was light of heart, thankful to have this time completely away from all responsibilities of work and family and expectant of what this time was going to provide. I was so full of experiences, content, new understandings, and things I wanted to remember for my work that I kept having to pull off the road to capture the thoughts. The flood continued to come and the depth of connection grew deeper and deeper the further I left the dilapidated porch behind and added filament after filament to the Heavenly Front Porch.

As I drove towards the area where the chapel was located, I left the last village and began going "back yonder" further and further into the mountains. I had both printed directions and the map on my cell phone to guide me, and there was a huge disconnect. I couldn't find it. My frustration began to grow, because I had felt so drawn to this chapel, and yet, I had a time frame to operate within to reach the retreat on time that night. I stopped at a little country store on the side of the road and asked some locals if they knew how to get there. I got a bit of the, "Go back about a mile, turn at the tree, go along for a bit and then…" I tried. I really did try to follow the local knowledge, but I was unsuccessful. That's when I observed something creeping onto my front porch. It was slimy and slithery and had as its sole purpose to keep me in a dilapidated state. I started being tempted not to finish the journey, to take the easy path and just go off to my final destination for the day, and I was able to observe that this was what was occurring in the moment. I fought it off and stopped at a second place to ask for directions again. This time, an old lady knew exactly where I was headed and told me to look for the next hard surface road off to the right named "x" and what to do as soon as I crossed the river. As I was leaving, I heard a man speak that I had not seen when I came in. He was sitting in the corner, and he reinforced some of the directions as I left. Thank goodness, as the next road to the right was hard surfaced and the correct road but without a sign.

With a determined mindset, I crossed a small stream, turned left and started driving back on a narrow country road that followed the river. Soon an enormous lake appeared on the right, and I thought about how wonderful it would be to have a home there in the peace of the mountains. Traveling along, I began to wonder if I was ever going to get there, as I had no sense of how long it was going to take me. Finally, way above the road on the side of the hill, I caught a glimpse of a beat up sign with sparse lettering. Had I not known what I was looking for, I would have missed the sign. The right turn was a steep angle back up the hill; so sharp that you could not turn onto the road from where

I was below. I drifted past and found a tiny driveway on the left that I could turn around in and came back pulling straight onto the incline and headed up. The website had indicated that the climb to the chapel was steep, and I was still blindly confident I'd be OK.

I am now way, way, way back in the mountains, alone, and driving to a meeting with my Boss that I didn't want to be late for or miss. As I started the climb, it was uphill but in an expanse of some open field for a bit, so I thought, "This will be OK. It's just a climb on up through some clear cut areas." Then, it started closing in, and I traveled through a square entrance of logs that had the look of a ranch welcome arch. As the all-wheel drive continued pulling me up, the road narrowed, the gravel got deeper, and as it turned to the right up the side of the mountain, the drop off got steep. There was no way to stop and go back. There was no place to turn around, and with the depth of the gravel, I dared not slow for fear of getting stuck. I also dared not speed up for fear of spinning out and off the side. The temptation not to complete the journey now shifted into fear of having started the journey and my failing confidence in my ability to finish it safely.

The mountain didn't yield to my shallow breathing and clinging grip on the steering wheel. It continued unfolding one switchback curve after another, going up steeper and steeper. I felt committed, but I didn't know to what or to what outcome, and I was scared. After the last fork to the left, suddenly there were two signs before me, but with the fog my brain was settling into from the stress as I worked to keep a steady speed, I wasn't able to read them quickly enough to know for certain what direction to take. I chose one last razorback to the right and kept throttling up to one last turn to the left. Suddenly, I was at the top, the very top of the mountains in the back ranges. I was alone.

Once I stopped my car, it had that slight smell of over-heating that announced it was not going anywhere for a while. There was no cell phone service. There was one house below me, but there was no sign of life. Of course, given my reaction to my entrance into the wilderness, I was in need of biological services. I parked my car next to a small one-room welcome center. I could literally see the restroom with its door open, but the front door was locked. I was uncomfortable in every way possible and started breathing deeply to try to calm the anxiety that had wracked my body during the climb. Focusing on anything other than a biological break was very hard to do. I was distracted and frustrated that after all the effort to get there, I wasn't able to be at peace and have the experience that I had intended for this trip. Yes, my focus was placed on what "I" had intended.

I decided to find the Chapel and at least see what I had come to see. At this point on the journey, "with Whom" I had come to be was missing. In a small field, there was another square log archway that I walked through on a dirt path. To the left was a small log cabin for silent retreats and to the right was a covered bench.

The quaint and beautifully constructed chapel was below the rise of the hill in the field and suddenly appeared from roofline on down to the foundation as I approached. A log was placed in front of the door, which has to be rolled away in order to enter, an interesting analogy in and of itself.

Inside the log chapel, there were four window bays with rocking chairs and prayer kneelers. The pews were all half-hewn logs, and behind the altar was a floor to ceiling glass window that displayed the vista across the bowl of the mountains. Continuing to be uncomfortable, I walked around and had a quick look. It's lovely. That's nice. I took a few photos and walked out highly unsatisfied. Strolling back to my car, I saw a side door to the welcome center and decided to try one more time to see if I could get in. Success! It was unlocked!! One more barrier was removed from my quest.

However, the battle continued for me to keep my appointment. So far, logistics, fear, and physical discomfort all had been tools to keep my porch in its dilapidated state. Each required a decision to name it as an invalid excuse and action in the form of persistence to press on and behave contrary to what was being presented.

The next deterrent came in the form of the elements. It started raining, and I started thinking about whether or not I was going to go back into the chapel, or if I was going to leave with the mission incomplete. I had gone on the journey. I had shown up. I had answered the call, but I had not listened yet. Suddenly, I realized that I was continuing to be both tempted and tested about whether or not I was going to be present. Was I going to stay on the dilapidated front porch, or was I going to connect to the Heavenly Front Porch?

As a menacing storm gathered on the mountain, I decided to return to the chapel with absolutely no idea why I was there. I had simply seen an article in a magazine and thought, "I have to go there." Back I went, moved the log, and entered a much darker chapel as the clouds sank over the mountaintop. I walked to the right and went to the first rocking chair and kneeler to pray, hoping to begin trying to figure out why I was there, to be quiet, and to hear. The kneelers had a short lectern with a Bible on them and a pillow at their base. I knelt down and started trying to pray. The pillow began sliding off. Back I put it, knelt again, and it slid off without a lip to hold it in place. I couldn't even pray in comfort and peace!

I stayed unsettled and began to walk around this small chapel. I looked at the view out each window. I took some more photos. I wandered back and looked at the materials on the table near the door. I signed the guest book. I circled the rough-hewn pews, around and around and around, as if I was walking a cathedral labyrinth. Looking for that soul-centering calm, nothing was working. As I paced, the clouds became oil-soaked cotton in their appearance. They closed in on the mountaintop. The winds threw themselves at the chapel windows, and they shook as the rain hit so hard it sounded like diamonds being thrown at the windows. Solo. No one. Nothing. Alone. In the middle of the chaos, I literally looked at my watch and said, "Alright, God. You've got thirty minutes." Clearly, this was my feeble attempt to take control of my fear and set boundaries on how long I was willing to be present and endure the discomfort, not to mention a demand to know His plan's timeframe and why I was there. All set new levels of arrogance as I sat on my dilapidated front porch.

It's in those moments of utter base human interaction with the Heavenly Front Porch that humor and grace show up. I knew in a second how ridiculous my behavior had just been. Finally, in a humble log chapel created by people who answered a calling in pure faith, I sat on the front log pew and fell into what can only be described as the deepest meditative prayer I have ever been in, nothing similar before or since. I don't know where I went, but it was a tight connection to the Heavenly Front Porch. When I came to, I moved over to the bench near the front window and sat looking out at the ranges of mountains, so close that I could easily have walked quickly to the left range or the right. I still hadn't heard a reason for why I was there, but I was calmer as the storm heaved itself at the chapel. Going anywhere wasn't an option so He had me. I had to decide whether to stay, get out of the boat, and trust Him.

All of a sudden in the middle of the black and gray, a light shaft came down on the left range and began broadening, moving along lighting up that side of the mountains as it went. I turned away for a moment, and it stopped. When I looked back, it started moving again, expanding along the mountains. I noticed, because light has been used before in my life accompanied with very specific messages. I heard clearly, "Don't leave in the middle of the storm. It's the most dangerous time for you."

Utter clarity broke through as I realized the metaphor for the day and my current situation. If I had found the chapel at the first attempt, I may have come and gone before the storm, and its messages would have been unavailable to me. If I had not pressed on and been determined to see the mission through in obedience by asking multiple people for directions and avoiding the temptations and test to quit, I would have missed the instructions for how to care for my dilapidated front porch. If I had left the chapel the first time when I wanted to just check the box that I had showed up, but not waited for the lesson, I would have been trapped in a violent and dangerous storm going back down the mountain in a car that was not ready to keep me physically safe. If I had not stayed and completed the calling, I would have missed the message that was to keep me out of harms way, connected to the Heavenly Front Porch and off the dilapidated front porch in the months to come. His plan. His perfect timing. His calling. Our response, "Hear I am,"[20] if only for thirty minutes. He got forty-five!

Every woman with whom I have shared this story has said, "You were on your OWN??!!!" No, I wasn't on my own. I allowed my earthly fears to try to convince me that I was on my own. I was with the best road trip Navigator we can have in life.

To close the loop on this story, the retreat provided opportunities to stay in a deep place of reverence, consultation, and co-creation. I was left with, "It's going to be fine," and the title for this book appeared during the journey. That being said, after the deep connection over three days, I didn't want to leave. I have a small inkling now of why people who have NDEs don't want to come back.

One week later, meeting with a significant encourager in my life, I declared, "I'm in my 'New Life,'" but in looking back at my notes on the journey, I had already declared I was in my new life as I started the trip. Two weeks later, another dear friend told me, "You're ready to fly. Unfold your wings." The messages started coming from all sides. I was open, listening, and anchored deeply to the Heavenly Front Porch.

The only thing keeping me sitting on a dilapidated front porch was my belief that I would not be enough instead of confidence that He was

---

[20] 1 Samuel 3:4, New International Version

enough and what He had for me was more than I could have designed on my own. Twice in three weeks, without knowing any of this story, a stranger and a long-time friend prayed for me to know that He had more planned for me than I could ever imagine. Two months later, a client did the same out of the blue. For the first time, I dreamed that I was praying and received insights on helping Christian business leaders around the country. New business models and partners began showing up that I would not have even thought to connect with or seek. I invite you to co-create porch to Porch and walk away from the dilapidated front porch.

SOUL SITTIN': SIMPLIFYING AND LISTENING

1. What are my stories of how I have **reconnected** with the Heavenly Front Porch **and renovated**?

2. What **journey have I not taken** yet that I need to go on?

3. How am I allowing people to **junk up my front porch**?

4. What **weeds have grown up** in my life so much that I can't even see my front porch? What actions do I need to take to remove them?

5. Is my porch dilapidated with **callings that are no longer mine**?

6. Where do I need to trim back the hedges around my front porch so I can see **how it connects to the Heavenly Front Porch**?

7. What is **holding me back** from living a full front porch life?

8. Where am I **setting time limits for God**?

9. What **new boundaries** do I need to establish to clean off my dilapidated front porch so it's ready for the next calling?

10. Who is being used to provide **messages of reinforcement** to me regarding my path?

11. What does God have to say about the **state of my front porch**?

SOUL SITTIN' TIPS:

1. Identify a weekend in the next six months when you can step aside from all commitments and examine the state of your front porch. It can be completed in many forms and is best done on your own. For safety, let someone know your plans and how they can reach you. Here are some options to help you think about creating a Soul Sittin' Retreat.

    a. Remain at home with the agreement of family to stay with relatives or friends or go on their own adventure. Recognize that the temptation to be distracted and not stay focused on the purpose of your retreat is more difficult when not breaking the physical routine of being at your home.
    b. For those who crave sand beneath their feet and beautiful sunsets, go to the beach.
    c. Plan a hiking weekend in the mountains or just hang out in a cabin.
    d. Go to your favorite hunting lodge or fishing stream.
    e. Return to a place that brings you peace.

In advance:

1. Commit to not turning on the TV and staying off of social media and the phone.

2. Decide what you would like to accomplish.

3. If you include activities in your weekend, be watchful for these to become an excuse not to go deep.

4. Create a plan or an agenda for what you will do:

   a. Pray, read the Bible, review your goals for the last quarter, and create new goals for the coming year.
   b. Think about things you need to move off of your front porch.
   c. Decide what renovations need to happen in your life.
   d. Stay open, and listen for the messages for you.
   e. Remember that this is just a framework, and be open to going on the journey as it appears.

   If done in a retreat setting with others, consider selecting one that has plenty of space provided for alone time on the agenda.

2. If you have recently completed a retreat experience, set aside 30 minutes once a week to review the notes you made while in that state. Examine the expectations you set for how you would be different following the retreat and how you are doing on progress. Take note of where different attitudes, behaviors, and listening have made a difference in your life. Keep track of what is occurring, and keep returning to the Heavenly Front Porch for ongoing guidance.

SOUL SITTIN' BLESSING FOR RENOVATIONS

"For I know the plans I have for you....plans to prosper you and not to harm you, plans to give you hope and a future." [21]

I've taken a look at my front porch, and it's not something I would post a photo of at the moment. It looks like I have allowed things to get into a state of dilapidation that is beyond a little clean up. I may need to acknowledge that it's time for some major renovations. I also may have stepped in there and been running away with things on my own without checking in on what You have for me to do. There is a possibility that I've not been listening very frequently either. I think it may be time for me to step back and survey the perimeter, take stock of how I let it get into this state, and listen for where You want me to go. Remind me "'silent' and 'listen' are spelled with the same letters." [22]

I admit that I'm tempted not to even start this review process. It's likely once we start out on the journey, I may look for an escape hatch and try to ditch this journey altogether. If I'm going to arrive at the top of the mountain, it's going to require some help on Your part to keep my resolve in place that this is the right time and that You're calling me to do this. In my weakness, I need to know that You've got this and that there is a plan that we're going to work through together. I may not like the state of my dilapidated porch, but it's where I've been most recently comfortable.

---

[21] Jeremiah 29:11, New International Version
[22] Author unknown, http://www.quotegarden.com.

I could be tempted to stay there without completing the renovation that I know deep down inside results in a better outcome than my reticence will produce. Stay with me, keep at me, and guide the construction of the next iteration of me.

"You who dwell in the gardens with friends in attendance, let me hear your voice!"[23]

THE OVER-FLOWING FRONT PORCH: LIVING IN COMMUNITY

While periods of solitude and reflection are important disciplines necessary to hear our calling, our front porch throughout our lives is meant to be full of God, family, and friends. We are supposed to be in relationship, living in community, sharing, helping, caring, and receiving.

When I was in college, I had the blessing of attending a church-affiliated women's college that was dedicated to helping women develop their potential and seek their calling. On the one hand, it was the era of the

---

[23] Song of Songs 8:13, New International Version

misnomer that women could, and should, be Superwomen. Having it all was defined as being fully able to give 100% to God, a husband, children, and a top-level career. Only that would have been 400%, and no one has 300% to spare. That being said, we were shaped by our motto "Not to be served but to serve" and encouraged to live noble lives as global citizens.

To that warm environment of learning and expectation, three women from Virginia came ready to tackle the as yet unveiled potential of our lives and to have the gift of a community that embraced our journey surrounding us. Under the protection of a campus that aligned with God through a President of strong convictions, a chaplain, and services on campus, we were able to have our beliefs and values challenged intellectually, our brains expanded, and our souls refined. When we had breaks from our studies, some conglomeration of relatives or friends would take one or more of us back and forth to Virginia.

We grew together and yet in completely different directions. Rosemary was sunshine any time she walked into a room. She had a laugh and a smile that could warm the most frigid December day. Rosemary chose to spend her spare time bringing joy to those in nursing homes. One can only imagine the many lives she would touch with her special gifts of charm, personal caring, and nurturing. Michelle was honing her business knowledge and was ready to take the world on by capturing the attention of a major tech company when they first came to our growing city with their new operations. She applied for a job in the purchasing department, got it, and then realized she *was* the purchasing department. Her corporate star was set to travel through the sky at dizzying heights. I thought I was on my way towards an academic career, but you'll hear later that God had other plans.

In September after our May college graduation, I was due to move to England for a year. Prior to leaving, I drove to Charlotte for a week to see my friends who had stayed in the area. Michelle and I enjoyed a visit together. She was happily ensconced in her new apartment and enjoying the challenges of her first corporate job. Michelle was starting to live the dreams that would make use of her God-given talent. She was an overt believer in God, trying to live her life under His guidance. We wished each other well, knowing that we wouldn't see each other again until I returned the next fall after completing my master's degree.

I arrived at the university in England, a large multi-college and international campus, as the only American Southerner they had ever enrolled. After a weekend Rotary briefing of all the ambassador scholars, classes began in my medieval studies degree program with a relatively small cohort. The academic rigor was intense so I threw myself into the routine of getting established in a new educational system, a different culture, getting to know my colleagues, and trying to figure out how to be successful.

Three weeks into this new endeavor, I was over any homesickness and happily adjusting to a new way of life. In mid-October after a long day of classes, I walked the couple miles from the Centre for Medieval Studies in the middle of the city back to the campus. A note was stuck to my door that indicated I needed to call my Dad. Now, first of all, my Dad calling was an alarm bell. We have always had a marvelous relationship, but neither of us is fond of phones. Secondly, there was the time difference and a phone box in the student common area that liked to eat a lot of coins. At the appointed time, I returned the call and learned that Michelle had been driving on her way to make her first professional presentation. An unlicensed driver hit the van pulling a boat in front of her, and she plowed into the center of the accident with such force that she wound up in the back seat and was killed. Needless to say that was one of the most difficult phone calls of my life and none-the-less easier for my Dad.

Two months to the day later, on December 14th, Rosemary and a friend were driving to pick up someone at the Denver airport in a snowstorm. She was killed in an accident with a snowplow. By December of the same year we graduated, I was the only one of the three of us still alive.

Up until that point, my front porch had been over-flowing throughout my life. I grew up with a loving family and knew all four of my grandparents, my great aunt, and my great-grandmother. I had magical visits to the family farm, spent childhood summers with my Mom's parents, and lived at a campground as a teenager each summer where my Dad held Sunday services and my family ran recreation for the campers. In high school, I continued life's path with many of the same people I had been to school with since kindergarten, was successful academically, enjoyed being a cheerleader, and experienced the normal teenage challenges. College brought a new full front porch of friends and gave me a protected environment in which to expand my views of the world and life. Going to England was a way of experiencing these newfound understandings in a foreign environment, while adding to my community of friends that I still visit regularly 30 years later.

Until that fall of double tragedy, it was the loss of my great aunt, great grandmother, and a grandmother that had begun to prepare me for the ebb and flow of the front porch. Those experiences underlined the need to pay attention to cultivating a full earthly front porch along with the recognition that not everyone stays with you through your whole life for a variety of reasons. That fall was an absolute shock to me. Far away from my support system, I had to accept that I had lost two of the people from my front porch who had dreams that were unfolding, which were not going to be completed. I had to wonder why two people who had so much to offer the world in different ways had gone home to the Heavenly Front Porch so soon. Thirty years later, I still have no idea.

At the same time, a new friend showed up on my porch. When I did not attend class the next day, one of the women on my course who was living in the city came to my dorm room to find out why I was not there. Thus was born a friendship of the heart that brought into my life my dearest English friend, her parents, husband, children, and a very extended family that I still visit and treasure thirty years later. I learned that our front porches can stay full throughout our lives, and yet, some people will rotate on and off at different seasons. Some stay for the whole journey, but many go before us, or serve the time they are meant to with us and move on to other front porches.

My Dad recently went on a journey back to the church he had when I was born. He wanted to see the parishioners who were still living, many in their 80's and 90's; people who had filled his front porch and stayed in touch throughout 60 years, even though they were not able to visit each other's front porches often. Many he visited had already journeyed to the Heavenly Front Porch, and yet, he also had the blessing of bumping into a young man he had confirmed, a representative of the continuing bridge between the Heavenly and earthly front porches.

People surface in our lives to walk in partnership with us when the time is right, sometimes to just sit for a spell on our porch and other times to stay for a longer portion of the journey. I went to a meeting in an auditorium for my alma mater once, looked across the room, and saw a man whom I had never met; and yet, the thought passed through my mind immediately, "I know you." He turned, caught my eye, and with a big smile waved at me as if we had known each other for years. That was the start of a friendship that positively impacted my professional development, calling, and journey to authoring this book. He arrived in my life at just the time that I needed support, to be challenged, and to be validated that the journey my life is on was in fact on track. I call him my Encourager Angel.

There was a moment when he said to me, "Keep hitting the note. The people who need you will hear the note." A few weeks later, I was reading a book recommended to me by a friend who is a Brigadier General and the first female in US history to serve in combat at the strategic level. She suggested I read, *Jesus CEO, Using Ancient Wisdom for Visionary Leadership*, which contained the following, "You may have to search for it, but once you hit the harmonic "C" - the note that matches perfectly with your soul - you, God, and destiny will be one harmonious sound. And others will stop, perk up their ears, and begin to gather round."[24] Or as my Encourager Angel also said, "Don't cloak who you are." It was incredible to me that two people, who had only recently been brought into my life, and with whom a clear understanding co-existed of why we are doing the work we are focused upon, pointed me to the same understanding.

When we live in God's community, those who are meant to be on our front porch to share our journey show up in our lives when our spirits are intended to intersect. If we pay attention, we will see the patterns, can welcome people onto our front porches, and will know when we are meant to show up on theirs.

---

[24] Jesus CEO: Using Ancient Wisdom for Visionary Leadership, Laurie Beth Jones, 1995, p. 20.

SOUL SITTIN': WALKING IN PARTNERSHIP WITH GOD, FAMILY, AND FRIENDS

1. Who has been walking the journey with you from the beginning that is **bridging the front porches** of your life?

2. What purpose do you **ascribe to their presence**?

3. What would be **different about your life** if they were not on the journey with you?

4. How are you **honoring** them in your life?

5. Who has surfaced at key moments and provided the guidance, counsel, nurturing, or direction that has **informed your spiritual journey** in the short-term?

6. Think through your life to date and find your stories of **being in God's community**, not just when people showed up on your front porch, but also **when has He had you show up on theirs**?

7. Whose front porch do you **need to show up** on now?

8. If someone from your front porch was unexpectedly and permanently **removed from your front porch**, how would you go forward?

9. Taking the time to be **more aware of your journey**, how will you interact with human beings differently from this point forward?

SOUL SITTIN' TIPS:

1. Compile a list of the long-term porch sitters in your life - family, friends, and colleagues, and examine the role that each of them has played.

   a. Who has been FOR you?
   b. What have you learned from each person?
   c. Now that you're paying attention, what else could you learn from them?
   d. How have they blessed your life?
   e. What can you do to return the blessing to them?

2. Consider whose front porch you have been sitting on for the long-term, both family and friends.

   a. What role do you see yourself continuing to play?
   b. What value are you adding to this partnership?
   c. What blessing can you offer to them?
   d. Have you over-stayed your welcome?

3. Next time you are in a group of people, be aware that you never know whose front porch you may need to visit. Instead of immediately gravitating towards those you know, and with whom you may be most comfortable, listen for the nudge to speak to someone new. Step back and observe the room for a few minutes. Notice who may be in need of some soul sittin' for a spell with you and be confident that you are enough in the moment. Living in partnership with connected front porches sometimes means being present for others in ways that you could not have predicted. Just because you received an invitation to something doesn't mean that's the only reason you are meant to be there. Keep your eyes open for a chance to walk soul to soul.

SOUL SITTIN' BLESSING FOR PARTNERS

***"For where two or three are gathered in my
name, there am I among them."***[25]

Thank You for those You have brought onto my front porch throughout the years. I may only just be recognizing all the ways that they have blessed my life. I am overwhelmed now with the observation of the many traveling partners who have appeared in different ways through the years. Help me to treasure those who are present with me now so that if I experience their absence temporarily or permanently, I will have valued the front porch time we have had in a way that fills me with smiles and not regrets.

As I travel this journey, nudge me to notice those who need me to visit their front porches, whether for a short time or for a long stay. Help me not to do any front porch bypasses when you need me to be in partnership with family, friends, or strangers who need to sit for a spell. Make me a blessing to them in a way that improves their path and provides them with opportunities to do the same for others. In true partnership, help me to be a bridge to communion between the earthly and Heavenly Front Porches.

---

[25] Matthew 18:20 English Standard Version, Text Edition: 2011.

"You prepare a table before me in the presence of my enemies. You anoint my head with oil; my cup overflows."[26]

EMPTYING YOUR FRONT PORCH

In long ago days, "Come on in and sit for a spell" could be heard on a daily basis. The calling card was not just polite notification that someone had stopped by. They were a work of art and a reflection of the visitor and their social status. Dropping by was the way to spread the local news, to unobtrusively check in on people who might need a little looking after, and to promote community – a friendship chat, a house call from the doctor, a parish visit from the local preacher, or a courting couple – all played a role in caring for one another.

---

[26] Psalm 23: 5 New International Version

Of course, not everyone encouraged those visits. Some lived alone and preferred it that way. Others perceived inquiries as being nosy or gossipy. Still others didn't put furniture on the front porch to encourage someone to stop by for a while or left the table and chairs folded up in the corner sending a direct message to potential callers. They had emptied their front porches permanently.

When we're young, our porch is full and our cups spill over with options that we haven't even seen yet. Life is one full-on exploration and adventure crammed with possibility. Every person we meet could be a new playmate or someone who is going to introduce us to a new experience we might find fun or interesting. Any object could have innumerable uses from practical to imaginary. We jostle each other to get a seat at the table where the action is engaging. We want our place whether it's at the children's table or the adult's table. We're willing to sit anywhere and try anything. Our discernment has not yet developed.

Over time, our life experiences start filling up multiple tables. Some overflow with good and useful things that can be re-used in a variety of circumstances in the years to come. Others weigh us down. They have no purpose anymore, and yet we still lug them from place to place with us. We add more tables and fill them up with useless items and people that we should have released decades before. We carry them with us wherever we go. Others are long gone out of our lives, and yet we allow them to stay alive in negative ways. We talk to them as if they were active participants in our lives, and we carry grudges for what they did or failed to do. We allow them to walk our journey with us, and they don't even know they have gone on the trip. We may have folded up their chairs on our porch, but we have left all their dirty dishes on the table.

Spiritually, we haul this stuff around with us, and our table full of possibility diminishes, or worse, we fold it up completely. We allow others to define for us what our lives are going to be instead of seeking the table that has been set specifically for us with the bounty that was placed there for us to enjoy and to use in service of others. We can't even find our place at the table anymore and aren't sure at which table we're supposed to be seated.

One of the blessings of adulthood is having children around so you can watch their abandon to the whims of the moment, see the creative spark and their timeless joy, and observe the testing of boundaries. To them, there are none until they are established - some for safety, some for discipline, and some to promote unselfishness. A banquet is set at their table from which they grab one possibility per second and gorge with an appetite seemingly birthed from starvation.

At what point do we lose our appetite and begin to believe in scarcity instead of being channels of unending resources? When do we buy into cluttering up our tables with the garbage of others' impact on our lives, allowing it to be heaped onto multiple tables on our front porch? How long will we allow ourselves to lug this around creating a groaning sound from the floorboards of our porch? When will we open our table and chairs to the guests who provide sustenance in our lives and can help us tap into the richness that is there for us to parlay into good works? When will we silence the naysayers and dump the refuse off our tables?

I once heard a speaker at a conference talk about her shock when her husband, who traveled for work, didn't come home. He wasn't late due to unsavory activities. He wasn't delayed. He didn't stop by the office on the way home. He died while away on a trip, and he was never coming home again. Unprepared for an instantaneous change in her entire world view, she spent time not only grieving and trying to map out her new life, but she also noticed what needed to change about her front porch.

Recognizing in a new way that time was precious and how she spent the unknown remaining years of her life was something to design and treasure, she began assessing what was in her life, and more importantly, who was in her life. She made a determination that if anything and anyone was not value-added, she needed to make a change. This was not selfishness but awareness of the limitations created by any time, effort, or relationships that stole her maximum contribution and best use of her soul's days. Uncluttering her front porch became an immediate priority as she prepared to set the table for the next phase. An inventory commenced of what she had allowed to enter onto the very sanctuary of her home's entrance, and a purge was undertaken.

In order to co-create, there has to be an intention about it and space to do so. Sometimes actual space is needed. The physicality of creating room for the new can also be a representation of the mental space that is needed for something else to come into your life. Holding onto the past does not allow you to propel yourself forward. Acknowledging what was and keeping a memento is recognition of from whence you have come but not a definition of where you must stay or to where you must then go.

There is a table and a chair with your name on it that has an earthly and a Heavenly Front Porch residence. You already have a reservation with royalty and a seat saved for you. Are you saving one on your front porch for Him? Have you folded up your table and chairs? Is your front porch cleaned off for the next visit so that there is room? Are you ready to sit at the table?

SOUL SITTIN': PREPARING TO SIT ON THE PORCH AND AT THE TABLE

1. What or to whom am I holding onto that is **cluttering** my front porch?

2. When I let go of what I am clinging to, what is the **scope of possibility** that opens up in my life?

3. What **evidences of abundance** are present in my life now?

4. What **abundance could I create** if I de-cluttered my front porch?

5. How am I **limiting the options** in my life?

6. What am I willing to do to **open up my table** and accept an invitation to "sit for a spell?"

7. Who will I **invite** to my newly laid table with me?

8. What is my **timeframe** for laying the table and extending the invitations?

9. I have a **defined number of soul days** on the earthly front porch. What is the percentage of my remaining days that I am willing to be stolen by leaving my table and chairs folded up on my front porch?

SOUL SITTIN' TIPS:

There is a plastic kids' table, a metal folding table, a tiled kitchen table, a mahogany dining room table, and TV trays folded up in the closet. All of them have seats suitable for each experience.

a. The kids' table is in the shade on the screened-in porch and is a jumble of crayons, books, sippy cups, tape, glue, colored paper, cookies, glitter, beads, string, Legos, stickers, colored pasta, scissors, hole punchers, and candy.

b. The metal folding table is outside on the patio in the full sunlight with a hose, potting soil, trowel, rope, flats of pansies, a gardening book, and an iPad.

c. The kitchen table is next to the window with a view of everything that goes by in the neighborhood. It has school backpacks, newspapers, recycling, the remains of breakfast, unopened mail, a potted plant, and a stack of unread magazines.

d. The mahogany dining room table has a family heirloom silver centerpiece, crystal serving dishes, scented candles, a Belgian lace tablecloth, damask napkins, and polished seats in the depths of the house.

e. The scratched, bent, and ancient TV trays with cup holders are hauled out of the closet every night at dinnertime for the adults, while the children fling themselves on the nearest sofa or the floor with their dinner. There is just enough room for a plate, silverware, cup and a napkin.

1. Which table describes the table you sit at most often? Is it the right fit for what needs to be on your front porch as you continue your journey?

2. Which table has the most attraction for you and why?

3. Which table do you need to fold up and stop using to create abundance and possibility?

4. Which table do you need to clean off in order for it to be used in the way in which it was intended and to its most abundant purpose?

5. Which table do you need to start sitting at and pull onto your front porch?

6. Is there another table that you need to create that fits your space better at this point?

7. What else needs to be placed on it as you lay the table for your new life?

SOUL SITTIN' BLESSING AS WE LAY THE TABLE

"And God is able to bless you abundantly, so that in all things at all times, having all that you need, you will abound in every good work." [27]

Help me to sort through the tables of my life. Clean off the ones that still need to be there but have been cluttered up. Fold up the ones that no longer serve Your purpose for my life. Throw away the rickety one that I'm carrying around to no good end. Focus my sight on the one of abundance that has been hidden behind the others, which is set for a banquet on my front porch. I'm ready to stop hoarding the things that leave my table heaving with limitations and to seek those things you have for me that will enhance my ability to follow, lead, and serve. Help me to regain my appetite for possibility and to recognize that how I use each soul day either fills up the front porch and sets the banquet table for others or diminishes my capacity to enrich the lives of those around me.

---

[27] 2 Corinthians 9:8, New International Version

"In vain you rise early and stay up late, toiling for food to eat-- for he grants sleep to those he loves." [28]

TIME FOR THE FRONT PORCH:
CYCLES OF REST AND CELEBRATION

Why is it that all year long we yearn for that one week at the beach and a week at Christmas? We say to ourselves, "If I can just make it 'til…" as if our minds, souls, and bodies were meant to be on a journey of panting instead of a steady cycle of learning, contributing, and rejuvenating.

Watching nature is one of the greatest ways to learn life lessons, and yet, with more and more urban living in the world, we have become completely disconnected with how things work outside of a science class. Instead of watching chickens hatch, cows being born, and butchering

---

[28] Psalm 127:2, New International Version

our meat once a year, we run by the grocery store and don't even grab food to fix. We pick up something prepared in the deli section or fill up a plastic food bar container. The life that a significant portion of the U.S. led sixty years ago was still agricultural. Those who grew up that way knew the value of crop rotation to let a portion of the land lay fallow. After a hard day in the field at harvest time, front porch visiting was a way of life, dropping off a warm pie or sharing newly canned vegetables. People would be encouraged to "give yourself a breather," and plans would be under way for dances and county fairs to celebrate.

While the experiences may seem dated to some, they carry tremendous wisdom transfer for us today in just the ideas that there is a time for work and for rest and a time to gather and to celebrate. Harvest festivals dating back centuries are a great example of communities enjoying the fruits of their labors, experiencing peace of mind before the winter came, and expressing thanks to each other for the variety of contributions from neighbors to a successful season.

Nature has given us four different rhythms to keep us in tune: a time when the new springs forth, incubating like a sponge in water, a time of robust activity in the summer, a time of maturity, contribution and meaning in the fall, and lastly, winter's blessing of gentle rest and front porch sitting. As many recount, "Even God rested on the seventh day!"[29]

One of the dangers of our choice to live life at speed is not recognizing what we are caught up in and not requiring of ourselves that we stop for moments of rejuvenation. In that time of rest, we have the option to reflect and to see more clearly than when we are caught up in the

---

[29] Genesis 2:2, New International Version

"doing." Our opportunities for observation allow us to see others passing by and to notice what is occurring to which we can contribute, create anew, or respond. It allows us to catch the trends for innovation that we might simply miss. Most importantly, we can see where we need to be a blessing to others.

When we don't have cycles of restoration built into our lives, it often comes to us in the most unexpected of ways. Despite the excessive hours we put in, we are not mindful of taking the break that is needed in order to stay in top form. The incessant treadmill actually reduces our effectiveness, kills our productivity, and leaves us unable to bring our best self to the job.

Our bodies are another way that we can get the wake-up call. Sometimes it comes in the form of a cold or the flu, because we're worn down and susceptible. Other times, it comes in a more serious way - the leg injury that keeps us from being as mobile and makes us dependent on others for a while, the cancer that throws us into a completely different relationship with life, family and God, or the permanent change in our career with the loss of a singing voice or our sight that brings on a recalibration of what we are meant to do while on this earth.

Over two decades ago, I began experiencing pain and exhaustion on a daily basis, unexplained all over body pain. Some days it would focus in on one place. Other days it was in another. Sometimes, it was completely debilitating like I was a hundred years old with muscles that wouldn't move properly. Some days there was no energy at all or brain fog. Other times, I couldn't eat certain foods and then I could consume them again a few weeks later. Sometimes, the back of my head was tender and would scream pain at the slightest touch. Some mornings, the day started out great and then went downhill. Other times, I woke up and felt the surge of energy from childhood. There was no rhyme or reason for what was occurring, and I didn't "look sick."

I had always run a hundred miles an hour in my life. Learning for me was just like breathing, and school was a place that couldn't give me the material fast enough. If there was a committee, I was on it. If there was a chance to go somewhere and see something new, I was there. Every discovery was an adventure whether it was Camelot at the Mill Mountain Playhouse with my grandparents or traveling throughout Virginia at my request for my eighth birthday to see historic sites instead of receiving presents. By the time I was in college, I kept on going at an intense pace, taking more courses than a normal load and going to summer school at another university, while I also worked, so I could earn a double major. Of course, I was on the church clogging team and the bell ringers, while leading the college religious life committee and had about twenty families that I babysat for part-time. I see some of the early signs now of what was yet to be discovered, as I would come home and crash on breaks, thinking that it was just a side effect of a busy schedule.

A few years later, as I lay my head on my husband's shoulder with tears running down my face from the pain, I thought I was dying. I couldn't imagine that there could be this much pain and that it was not terminal. Secretly, I got my affairs in order, as I was certain that I must not have much time left. And then came the dual diagnosis – you have two chronic illnesses that will be with you for the rest of your life. One will create symptoms for you all your life despite medication. The other is a disorder, which you will feel every day of your life, and which will manifest itself differently, unpredictably, and painfully.

While overwhelming to hear, I have never forgotten my husband's reaction. He said, "We need to be thankful that it is not degenerative. We know now that your body has an internal barometer that tells us how you should live." On the one hand, when you've been given permanent diagnoses of devastating things to live with, you might think this is not as empathetic a response as one would anticipate. However, the lens with which he viewed the news immediately put everything into an action-oriented way of looking at life and confirmed that *we* were going to handle this together and that these diagnoses gave us information to learn how to manage life productively and positively. Our job was to pay attention and to learn together. He supported me without enabling me to see myself as a victim, and he did not leave me alone. His approach that we needed to be thankful that it was not degenerative was also a reminder to remember what blessings look like. Things can always be more difficult. While I had something tough to overcome, I still had the majority of my ability to function and could live a rich life.

The second thing that happened was that I realized that my body had defined for me that cycles of rest were crucial to my ability to perform at my peak for the rest of my life. Taking care of myself included learning how to exercise in a way that challenged my body but did not drain my reserves. Eating correctly wasn't a matter of vanity for weight management but essential for providing the right nutrients to give my body a fighting chance every day. Sleep wasn't something to cut short, because it was where your body gets the capacity to function at its peak each day.

Most importantly, I made a choice about what life was going to be once I learned I was not going to die soon from these conditions. It was a given that I was going to feel tired from non-restorative sleep and that I was going to hurt at different levels each day. That was going to happen whether I was lying in bed, going for a walk, traveling the world, or making a speech. I had "normal" redefined for me, and it was different from how I was at 16 when I could dance for three hours straight every Saturday night at our campground's country dances. It didn't mean I couldn't dance anymore, just not for three hours. I learned how to translate life into new circumstances.

Shortly after this, the opportunity of a lifetime appeared when an international association with over twenty-five thousand members in eight hundred chapters around the world offered me the CEO position at thirty. I wanted this shot more than anything and was confident that I could do this work. I applied, enjoyed the people during the interview process, and was hired. This was within weeks of being diagnosed. A huge low point was followed by an incredible high point in my career, literally just moments apart. Had I allowed myself to limit what was possible, instead of believing what was possible through Him, I would have missed a key linchpin in my life and tremendous experiences that occurred as a result.

Getting ready to take on the biggest professional challenge of my life was an enormous counter blessing to what I had just learned. It was an opportunity to be consumed by a new vision for my career, to put into action adjusting my life in a way that would allow me to handle a high stress, high profile position with significant travel, and it was also a test to see whether or not I would answer His call. Because I said, "Yes," doors opened to me for years to come by simply learning how to respond, trust, and learn the value of cycles of rest and celebration as part of God's blessings in my life.

SOUL SITTIN': RECLAIMING YOUR LIFE'S NATURAL CYCLES

1. Where in your life have you allowed your schedule to negatively inform the **quality of your life**?

    a. What steps are you willing to take to **eliminate these effects**?

2. What is your body telling you about **how you are living your life**? Do you need to pay attention to

    a. sleep,
    b. nutrition,
    c. exercise,
    d. noise in your surroundings,
    e. fun, play, diversions, or
    f. health in general?

3. Why have you neglected cycles of rest and celebration in your life?

    a. What do you **believe you are gaining**?
    b. What are you **sacrificing** by doing so now and in the future?

4. In the next month, how can you insure you have a weekly **period of rest** that involves only you?

    a. Who would be positively affected if you choose to **add this dimension** more to your life?

b. Who can **join you** in regular attention to rejuvenation that will enrich your experience?

5. **Where is your life**: in spring, summer, winter, or fall? Describe why you selected this season.

    a. Spring: Bursting forth anew and incubating like a sponge
    b. Summer: Energetic robust activity
    c. Fall: Maturity, contribution, and meaning
    d. Winter: Blessing of gentle rest and front porch sitting

6. **What season would you like** your life to be in now?

7. How will you **deal with any disconnects** between where it is and where you want to move it towards?

8. What will you gain by **sitting on the front porch** more regularly?

SOUL SITTIN' TIPS:

1. **Front Porch Rejuvenation Assessment**: Look at key facets of your life and determine what season each area below is in. Decide if this is where you want it to be. If not, identify where you want to evolve each area, prioritize them, and set one step for each that will move them forward.

   a. Health
   b. Education
   c. Marriage
   d. Children
   e. Parents
   f. Friendships
   g. Career
   h. Professional Development: Certifications, post-grad work
   i. Hobbies/Fun
   j. Faith and spiritual development

2. **Celebrating!** Think about what you could celebrate in your life right now. What have you rushed past that should be memorialized as an accomplishment? It does not have to be something as big as earning a degree or winning an award. Where have you broken a habit successfully that was not serving you well? When have you shifted time to something more beneficial to your family than something else that was occupying your time unnecessarily? What have you done that has improved your health? How have you changed priorities in little ways that are taking you down the right path?

   a. Identify your most recent successes in life.
   b. Decide whether you want to mark them privately or with family and/or friends.
   c. Select a time that allows you to relish in the positive changes that are allowing you to rejuvenate your life.
   d. Do something just for you that memorializes and reinforces the celebration while encouraging you to continue to make more strides forward.

SOUL SITTIN' BLESSING FOR REJUVENATION

"There is a time for everything, and a season for every activity under the heavens."[30]

I am exhausted from the doing. My head sloshes full of alphabet soup from the to do lists floating in it. I admit to being someone who has worn the neglect of me like a badge. I can't remember the last time that I took a Sunday afternoon for personal pursuits that fill my soul. Vacation has seemed like something else on the checklist instead of a time for rejuvenation. If it was just my schedule I could get under control that would be great, but it's the kids, the spouse, the boards, the charities, the church, the parents, and the friends.

Help me to recognize that the failure to take care of myself lessens my ability to fulfill the plan for me, to even see the plan for me, and to operate at my peak performance. I want to experience the seasons. I yearn for the freshness of spring and the sense of new horizons appearing before me that would allow me to stretch and create possibility. The bustling period of summer as it bursts into full bloom would be welcomed with excitement, knowing that the fruits of fall are shortly behind when I could witness the impact of the contribution. If that was followed by a winter of rejuvenation and celebration of accomplishments before the next stretch, I know I would be expectant as spring came back into my life. I'm ready to adopt the rhythms of life that keep me sustained and allow me to be a blessing.

---

[30] Ecclesiastes 3:1, New International Version

*"Now, I am ready to visit you for the third time,
and I will not be a burden to you, because what
I want is not your possessions, but you."* [31]

RETURNING TO THE FRONT PORCH

Our first home on the Heavenly Front Porch is as a child of God. Our blessings and sustenance come from Him. Listen to children speak of God, and it's a very simple matter of fact statement. If you haven't read Todd Burpo's *Heaven is for Real* or been exposed to the art and poetry of Akiane Kramarik, who was born to an atheist family and began painting pictures of Jesus and heaven at four, you have missed the opportunity to witness what living the verse of "unless you change and become like little children"[32] means.

---

[31] 2 Corinthians 12:14, New International Version
[32] Matthew 18:3, New International Version

As we enter the earthly front porch and the veil falls behind us, it requires us to make the effort to "phone home."[33] It necessitates creating habits that allow us to live parallel lives, or in our best lives, to pull as much of the Porch onto our earthly one as possible, to be in the world but not of the world.[34]

If we don't make the effort to stay tuned in, like an old radio, the dial gets turned and left at an awkward angle with static coating the true signal. Over time, the tuning device gets rusty and turning the dial back to align with the signal requires more effort. Meanwhile, the signal skips, fades, and our ability to hear it dies away. The effort it takes to clean the dial back up, to wrench it loose, and to hear the clarity of the sound requires even more of us than if we had stayed constant in our habit of listening for the sweet sounds. We have to make time on our calendar in even longer increments to clean up the mess than if it had been maintained. We must care for a very delicate instrument even more guardedly than we would have before. Our patience has to be honed back to a fine level from our laziness, because we've now created a real job for ourselves.

The irony is that we never stopped owning the radio. We never ceased the ability to turn it on. We were never blocked from the signal. The transmissions continued consistently coming to us trying to reach us. Our receivers got stopped up. We stuffed earbuds into our ears. We kept the TV on 24/7. We turned the radio on in our cars to drown out the signals. We began to process the sounds as white noise or to allow the world to diminish our desire for the music. We let our own thoughts take priority and lead us to a new channel.

---

[33] Mathison, M (Screenplay author). (1982) "*E.T.*" [Film]. Universal Pictures.
[34] Romans 12:2, New International Version

The good news is that the Heavenly Front Porch is crafted of eternal stability and never changes. The wood doesn't get termites and rot. It never needs a new coat of paint or waterproofing, and there are always enough chairs for everyone. The one with your name on it never moves. How long it stays vacant is your choice, but there is no distance that you can go that is so far away that He won't be standing there holding the back of the chair in honor of you as you come home and take a seat.

What does wandering away from the front porch look like? It's that old slippery slope of forgetting that we are children of God, already members of the best family that exists. In our forgetting, we go looking for the things that we think will make us whole and make us feel like we belong. So we take one step away trying to walk on our own, and we look back with a quick glance to see if anybody noticed that we've stepped off the porch. It's the kid that wants to run off to the stream below the house on his own when his parents have said, "We'll go later together," and the child misses that this means "under our protection and with the family" – the safest place you could be.

And then, we take another step and another, and soon, we stop looking back. We forget that while we have the free will to go wherever we want, the smart way to travel is the buddy system. The first time I wandered in this way, I still had one foot on the front porch. I did all of the things outwardly that looked like I was still connected fully, and yet it was like a game of tag. Run away from the front porch, test it out, and run back and touch the front porch. It was as if the sporadic touching was going to prevent the predictable poor choices from happening or diminish their outcomes, or as if partially listening to the parents was going to keep you from getting wet in the stream with the only set of clothes you had – or worse yet drowning.

The decision, and yes, it's a decision, to play this childish game only has one ending regardless of the storyline. If one doesn't leave these patterns behind, continuing to do so into full adulthood leaves devastation wherever you go, and it no longer affects just you. My Mom used to tell me that if I couldn't behave at home, there was no way that I would be going out, that the first measure of real freedom came in being able to treat those you loved most with respect and care. If our first home is the Heavenly Front Porch, and we don't treat it with tender regard, what can we expect from our lives on the earthly front porch? When the signal gets so faint that only a dog can hear it, we wonder what it's howling at and fail to realize it's not just the piercing sound but the wounding of the dog's heart knowing his master can't hear anymore.

So here I am, as a child of God, stepping off the front porch and forgetting that He is enough regardless of what comes my way. These pictures are from youth and show an inability to take my beliefs and live them in confidence knowing that He remains in control, that I don't have to be and that all I have to do is just ask. For me, this is the face of uncertainty when I was not fully on the Porch. This is not a commentary or judgment that every person who struggles with physical challenges is off the Porch, as there are many reasons, including medical ones, for our body's appearance. For me, I know I was off the Porch, experiencing the agony of wrestling with soul battles to let go and let God, which manifested in this way.

You know you have your faces of uncertainty when you have stepped away from the Porch that you can insert into a picture frame. The images have probably just popped into your head. They may not have dramatic physical differences, but they are from phases of your life that you can spot clearly on the inside. You know which ones they are just like I do.

My Face of Uncertainty when off the Porch

I selected a socially acceptable drug of choice – food in one phase and the lack of food in another. At the time, I didn't realize that was what I was doing, nor could I label it, although I did know that chaos was swirling. From the outside, it would have looked like, "What on earth are her problems?" She has made good grades through her entire academic career and been blessed with scholarships to cover debts. She has great parents who love her dearly. She has enjoyed all four grandparents, a great grandmother, and extended family. She was a cheerleader in high school, raised in the church, and experienced the blessing of travel. She has been teed up for life! Nothing really bad has ever happened to her. And yet, an inner attack on self-esteem, its downward spiral, a perception of a lack of control, and a sense of not measuring up to the world's definitions crowded in from all sides. Food as a coping mechanism was only one outward feature of the tapes that played around not being good enough and impacted all facets of life.

And so you might say, well how bad were your demons? You didn't come home drunk to your family abusing them physically or with vile words. You didn't have to go to rehab to get off drugs and remain vulnerable to them for the rest of your life. You didn't wind up in prison. No, I didn't. However, I did have to learn for the rest of my life how to use a drug of choice three times a day to stay alive, while controlling a coping mechanism that was the first call to me. I did have to decide that starving myself for the illusion of control was not the answer, though I wouldn't have responded that was what I was trying to do at the time. I did have to break out of a personal prison, which I absolutely could not do on my own. This is what it means to be a child of God and to come home to the Heavenly Front Porch, to surrender all that is driving you internally and externally and to learn to walk in trust and by faith. Real happiness lies in recognizing that the Plan is there. He's got it, and you don't have to try so hard - so hard to be enough, so hard to be liked, or so hard to know that you're going to be used in a valuable way throughout your life. Just return to the Porch and stay tuned in.

We are very fortunate that we get metaphors for this experience of returning home, in this case the prodigal son. I began the long, bone-throbbing, dirty, heaving for air walk back to the Porch, which

occurred over a period of years. I found my family having waited patiently for me, ready to sit on the porch with me in love, understanding, and renewal, with the chair that has my name on it pulled up near them. It was then that I decided, yes it is a decision, to stay on the Heavenly Front Porch. I committed to no tag touching for the rest of my life, to keeping the radio tuned to the signal emitting off the Heavenly Front Porch, to identifying that I am a child of God, and to accepting the adoption papers that had already been signed years ago. The moment of choice occurred when spontaneously praying from the depths of my soul:

> *"I'll go where you want and do what you*
> *want, even if it's not somewhere*
> *I think I want to be, if you'll just take my*
> *life and make something of it."*

SOUL SITTIN': ASSESSING YOUR LOCATION - WHERE ARE YOU?

1. When was the last time you **turned on the Heavenly radio**?

2. What is **blocking you from receiving the signals** from the Porch?

3. How can you **tune in the channel** for stronger reception?

4. Can you **remember** the last time you were fully sitting on the Porch and what brought you there? What has changed?

5. If you've been away from the Porch and returned, write **your story** of returning, and feel the **welcome home**.

6. If you're on the Porch every day, what **practices** keep you there? Record them so that you can **intentionally** remain there for the rest of your life.

7. Do you have only one foot on the Porch? If so, what are you willing to do to step onto the Porch and **sit in the chair with your name** on it? Write down some daily practices you are willing to undertake to move you onto the porch:

    a. I will **visualize stepping** onto the Porch and sitting down for a chat.
    b. I will remove my earbuds at least once a day and **replace them with the signals from above** that will keep me connected with the Porch.

    c.   I will find time at least once a day to acknowledge that I need to **practice returning to the Porch** and to seek guidance on how to stay there.

8.   Are you confident that there is a chair and that **you have an invitation**? If not, here is a simple prayer for you:

> Heavenly Father, I want to sit on the Porch with You. I know I have been away for some time and that You have patiently waited for my return. Thank You for saving me a seat and for having a chair with my name on it. I would like to sit down and rest for a spell with You. Please help me to sit in peace with You and to stay on the Porch while I also have to live on the earthly one at the same time.

SOUL SITTIN' TIPS:

1. If you need to return to the Porch, plan your trip.

   a. Acknowledge why you have been away and that you want to come back.

   b. Start walking. Just put one foot in front of the other.

   c. As you journey back, notice:

      i. What you pass along the way

      ii. The things that would have distracted you from finishing your journey before

      iii. The things that tempt you to stop now

      iv. What is different this time about returning home to the Porch?

   d. Decide that you're going to stay.

SOUL SITTIN' BLESSING IN PREPARATION FOR COMING HOME

"The Lord will watch over your coming and going both now and forevermore." [35]

Thank You that I have the opportunity to return to the Porch. Some days, I don't tune in very well, or I need to switch channels. Catch my attention, and turn up the signal to a squeal if I'm missing the transmission. Help me to recognize that I may be on the Porch in a lot of ways, but there may be other ways that I'm not even hanging on by a toe. Get me ready for my total return so that I am fully capable of completing what You have for me. Assist me in breaking out of any prisons in which I have placed myself. Let me feel that a welcome awaits me so that I can continue the return through the desert that I created for myself. Make me gracious in receiving the consequences of having left the Porch and full of thanksgiving for the opportunity to reside on the Porch again – this time forever. Replace my face of uncertainty with one full of trust and faith. I'm on my way. See You soon.

---

[35] Psalm 121: 8, New International Version

"But now the Lord my God has given me rest on every side, and there is no adversary or disaster." [36]

THE THREATENED FRONT PORCH

Once we've come home to the Porch, we can easily be under the illusion that everything is going to be perfect on the earthly front porch from that point on. We're connected and living under His will and guidance, so all is going to be one happy party. Sometimes the elation of our welcome home party glow can last for a long time, which creates a special vulnerability requiring watchfulness. We think it's always going

---

[36] 1 Kings 5: 4, New International Version

to be smooth sailing, because we're safely ensconced in our Porch chair, doing the ritual of our best spiritual practices, while we are being and representing the Porch as we think we should.

We forget that we live day to day on the earthly front porch, that others have less than glorious designs on our time here, and that life is rarely smooth for lengthy periods. Other times, the afterglow gets snuffed out very quickly as reality delivers illness, a loved one dies, a lay-off affects our security, or a child makes poor choices. The Porch gets replaced with gates to our hearts, ears, time, and souls. Therein lies our option of whether we step off the Porch on our own, or recognize that when someone wants to burn down your front porch, you can sit strongly in your Porch chair and weather the attack with the best back up we could ever call upon.

We used to live in a cedar-sided country colonial with a wrap-around porch, corner tower and side screened-in porch. My husband loved his outdoor living with a passion, while I moved out of the melting mid-state heat into the cool of the air conditioning most of the time. One day, I heard that tone in his voice that every spouse recognizes as a combination of great puzzlement and great danger. When he called my name, I leapt two landings of stairs to the first floor in almost one stride and was outside in a streak of concern. Leaning against the porch railing and with a paralyzed question mark, he said, "Cynthia, why is smoke coming from the ground?" Not having a clue, when my husband asked, "What do we do?" I said, "We call the firemen!"

We learned that someone had buried inside wiring for an outside light pole, ran it into the house, and failed to install it through a conduit. It was slowly burning its way to the crawl space under the house where it was coiled in position to burn our home down. Our front porch was being assaulted, and we needed the cavalry of firemen and an electrician to stop it. When you're under attack and your earthly front porch is threatened, it requires us to call in those who can surround us with the skill set needed in the moment, wise counsel, emotional support, and a selfless care for us. In other words, sometimes we need our earthly front porch community.

I was out for my prayer walk one morning, and I saw an exceedingly large hawk on the front porch of a lot of other birds' homes in the city, an unusual sight in our neighborhood. It wasn't long before the alarm went out among mockingbirds and cardinals in the vicinity that their front porch was in danger. Each individual nest was vulnerable, and no bird knew exactly which would be attacked. However, they all helped each other to minimize the potential tragedy to the entire community. Being with others who know how to spot what could be on your threshold is critical for a life remaining on the Porch.

Sometimes once you have been on the Porch for a period of time and have proven yourself to be ready for use, the challenge that comes your way has to do, not with your earthly front porch, but with someone else's front porch at risk. Those battles are particularly wearying and can last for a long period of time. Being ready to "put on the full armor of God"[37] is a necessity to withstand the attacks that will inevitably come your way. The earthly rewards for enduring them may not be forthcoming, and one must be ready and willing to forego them. The efforts put forth are not

[37] Ephesians: 13-18, New International Version

for you but for Him and to give others the opportunity to reconnect with the Porch in an authentic way.

I once served with a team who had an option to be transparent about an unfortunate issue that was before us. The decision was made to restrict the conversation from others who had a right to know the circumstances. After consulting trusted advisors, I held the space open for a different conclusion to be reached, knowing that in doing so there was a strong likelihood by simply taking this action there would be a negative consequence to me. On the earthly front porch, there was an ego force field of attraction to walk away and join the crowd. However, I would have always known that I stepped off the Porch and received personal gain from doing something that was not in alignment with the Porch. The choice was taken to continue on the same path. The objection was made, and the personal price paid.

During that experience, I knew that I had the support of a strong Christian team backing me, and my faith was present as I challenged people whom I respected. A world-view was broken for me on that day. As I struggled with the experience, from an unexpected colleague, I received strong reinforcement, "I think God is protecting you." I learned that not everything should be perceived as a personal price when, in fact, it might very well be the best thing that could happen from the Porch perspective. I have the comfort of knowing that in this case, I stayed firmly in my seat when my earthly front porch was threatened, though that does not mean that I wasn't tempted to step off of the Porch.

To be clear, the threats don't stop coming. The more you become comfortable in that Porch chair, the more threats will come your way.

No sooner had I gotten past the eating disorder, learned to live well with chronic illnesses that create physical pain, and stepped into "I'll go where you and do what you want," it was time for the next big attack. The place where I had always had my success was from my mind. Identified as a gifted child in second grade, I excelled in any subject, loved reading and writing, could absorb anything quickly, lived in eternal curiosity, and absolutely loved learning. While I set out to be an academic and had plans to finish a doctorate, God diverted my path and plan, and I wound up being the CEO for national and international organizations. My gifts were in business turn-arounds, leadership, developing people, speaking, change management, board governance, strategic planning, simplifying very complex systems, teaching, and leading large groups; all of which required extensive travel.

Prior to what should have been a very enjoyable business trip, a doctor pulled me off the only medication I take in order to temporarily readjust a level. I begged the physician not to do this before a trip to no avail. As a result, I had a medical crisis on the plane returning home, which required the plane to land. New physical symptoms developed, which affected my body for years. It created the worst decade of my life. I also had a reaction to the event that was connected to flying, which created anxiety for years. Every time, I stepped into a plane, the attacks would begin from the point of sitting down to the sound of loading luggage, shutting the door, revving the engine, and going down the runway. It was heart breaking, because I had always loved to go and loved the excitement of adventures. The feelings would start in my feet and travel all the way up affecting my heart rate, my breathing, and my ability to sit still in the seat. All I wanted to do was run down the aisle to get off.

This experience repeated itself flight after flight after flight for years until I learned a new set of skills and to write long-hand, sometimes for hours at a time, to get me from one place to another. I should have started this book then!

Nobody but my husband knew the fight that was on when I got into a plane to fly to Italy, Scandinavia, Brussels, Oslo, England or the Netherlands; or the eight days when I flew back and forth across the U.S. every other day to make presentations and consult. Over time, I completely conquered what was a direct attack on my mind and therefore my ability to use my gifts to their fullest. I was only able to continue through prayer, my husband's support, practical tools, and the will not to be taken out from the work that had been assigned to me from the Porch. Imagine experiencing terror before you begin to do whatever your normal work is every day and fighting through that with your energy being consumed in a negative way. That is what it felt like every time I flew, which in many cases was multiple times a week. Unfortunately, once the pattern was established, it was not restricted to flying and could come on in any environment at any time.

I had a choice, as we all do, whether or not to take up my calling. I could have chosen disability payments at the point of the chronic illnesses. I could have chosen to just coach from my bedside and not take any consulting appointments or not accept another position requiring travel.

However, I chose to sit on the Porch with His hand on the back of the chair marked for me and to step out with the full armor of God, not because I'm anything great, but because I am able to "do all things through Him."[38] I am incapacitated in life without Him. He led me to the tools I could use to overcome the anxiety attacks and to the best doctor for the chronic illnesses that I could have possibly found as I searched for relief. Each step is an amazing story of God's intervention in and of itself, too many to include here, but so reinforcing when you examine the threads of your life's story and see the pattern of God's handiwork and your palm resting in His.

Even as I wrote this book, it's been interesting to observe what happened. On the one hand, people of great encouragement showed up to support and encourage. Out of the blue, a dear friend who has connections with a celebrity received a call from that individual's spouse to let her know of a Christian speakers and writers conference being held within twenty minutes of the house. It has been going on for years and neither of us knew about it. That experience created the opportunity to meet and learn from publishers and writers. On the other hand, the more I wrote, the more physical challenges reappeared and stole time. My printer died. The new laptop started acting up in ways it had not before. When I needed solitude to write, someone decided to start running machinery outside. A couple of days, the double vision that can plague me set in for several hours each morning. Distraction after distraction after distraction appeared. The more you plant yourself firmly on the Porch, the stronger the attacks will get.

There are no guarantees that your front porch is not going to be threatened. It's about what you do when it *is* threatened. My desire for those who have chosen to go on this journey is to know as early as

---

[38] Philippians 4:13, New International Version

possible that life is one long journey of co-creating with God. The sooner that you do that willingly every day, all day long, the easier that it gets to stay planted on the Porch, especially when it's threatened. Don't test it. Don't have one foot on and one off. Don't run away from it and then come back and tag it. Stay on the Porch.

Photo with kind permission of Lindsey Ocker
Photography at LindseyOcker.com

SOUL SITTIN': TURNING TOWARDS THE HEAVENLY FRONT PORCH

1. Consider your story. When have the legs of your chair been **wobbly on the Porch**?

2. How are you **prepared for your next response** when your front porch is attacked?

3. How will you **know that you are ready**?

4. What **behaviors and practices** will you exhibit?

5. Is there a shadow on your chair that is **preventing you from seeing the light** from the Porch?

    a. **Where are you sitting** - on the lighted or shaded side of your front porch? We do get to choose.

    b. If you could **make one change now** in your choices, what would that be?

6. What may be **threatening your front porch** in the months ahead?

7. How will you **plan to remain strong**?

8. Are you under attack now? **What is at stake**?

9. **Who can you call** upon to strengthen you during this time?

10. Is there anything you should **walk away from now**?

SOUL SITTIN' TIPS:

1. Write down two or three times **when your front porch was threatened** and how you responded.

    a. When did you succeed in **remaining firmly planted** on the Porch?

    b. What were you **practicing, clinging to, or praying for** that allowed you to stay solid?

    c. When you weren't as successful, **what was missing**? Was it intentional, lack of awareness, under-development, or was it sloppy living?

2. Find a visual representation to put on your iPad, carry with you, put up in your room, display in your office, or see wherever you spend your time that can remind you of the **need to protect your front porch** while remaining firmly seated on the Porch.

SOUL SITTIN' BLESSING FOR PROTECTION

***"The Lord will keep you from all harm
– he will watch over your life."*** [39]

Sometimes Your assignments are tough. My front porch gets threatened in ways that make it very uncomfortable here. It's hard to stay seated on the Porch with You. There are things that I want out of this life that I think I have earned and should be mine, but they threaten my safety on the porch. Thankfully, You declare them not to be for me. When that occurs, let me accept it, act accordingly, and be thankful instead of resentful. Help me to always trust that You have my best interests at heart, that You will stand with me when my porch is threatened, and that You will provide the support I need in order to complete the work You have for me to do.

---

[39] The Bible, Psalm 121:7, New International Version

*"For I am persuaded, that neither death, nor life,
nor angels, nor principalities, nor powers, nor things
present, nor things to come, nor height, nor depth, nor
any other creature, shall be able to separate us from
the love of God, which is in Christ Jesus our Lord."*[40]

THE FRONT PORCH HAVEN

There is nothing about living a modern life that provides a sense of
peace in our daily existence unless we seek it. Our society rewards
being in constant motion, and in the U.S., people wear not taking a
vacation like a badge of honor. As we tread this path, we wear our feet
to blistered pulp. Our hearts leak. Our ears throb with the constant

---

[40] Romans 8: 38-39 King James Version

pounding input, and our minds are chaotic from incessant toing and froing. We are unable to handle the blessing of silence and what can appear in that space.

If we give ourselves permission to spring into reverence instead of activity, we have the opportunity to find solace. There come times in our lives when we don't even know that the front porch is missing. We've forgotten that there is this safe location attached to our homes. We forego the invitation to come and sit, and we keep at it on our own. We fail to invite those who can sit with us to share our journey. We stop connecting to the Porch and create expectations of ourselves that are not in line with the purpose for our lives. Then, we wonder why the resources don't show up to support them and puzzle about why we flail at life trying this and then that. Nothing seems to work.

As we inch our chairs further and further away on the front porch, and then off the porch altogether, we wind ourselves up into a trap of ego and perfectionism. "I have to do this, and this, and this. It has to be like that and that. My way is the only way this is going to turn out well." We can never attain what we set ourselves up for, excellence yes, but perfectionism no. It's our internal desires that turn us away from the daily haven. We have access to it if we will but turn towards the Porch, pick up our chairs, take their assigned place, relax into the promises, and recognize the haven.

There have been several times in my life when the front Porch has shown up and a vivid understanding that I was living under His wing was presented to me. A particularly vivid occurrence happened when I was concerned that what was going on in my body could lead to an early death. I knew that it was time for the answer regardless of the outcome and my fear. After going to a series of doctors, I was awaiting the final results. I continued to live my life, which included travel for work. I was in the airport bookstore looking for something to read on the way home, when I saw a magazine cover with an article titled something like "Are you tired of feeling constantly tired?" It struck a deep chord of knowing in me that scared me, and I moved away from it. I heard, "Pick it up." Not an audible voice but very clear. That was the first time this had happened to me in this way, and it startled me. I instantly soul-reacted and responded with an attitude, "I don't want to pick it up," and I moved away again. With more urgency and demand in the tone, I heard again, "Pick it up." I said again, I don't WANT to pick it up." And then with a roaring command, the voice pronounced, "PICK IT UP!!!!!" I snatched it off the stack as if my visible actions were going to be seen by someone standing there, bought it, and stormed out angry. I felt as though I had been Jacob wrestling all night long.[41]

On the plane, still sulking over losing the battle, I responded with almost an "I'll show you" reaction by reading every other alternative I had but the magazine with that article in it on the long flight home. Finally, I caved and started reading. My health experience was in every word of that article. At last, I had a name for what I had been going through, and I wasn't going to die. It wasn't going to be easy, but I would live. When I returned to the doctor's office for the test results, I interrupted him mid-sentence, as he was getting ready to share what he had learned. I said, "Do I have…?" He responded, "Yes you do, as well as…" In that moment, I realized that I had been granted a haven from the shock of what would be shared. I had been protected, not from the journey and what it would teach, but from the jolt of the result. This was pre-internet

---

[41] Genesis 32: 22-31 New International Version

so the options for learning on your own were limited. The delivery had been gentle and a relief in so many ways, was processed in privacy, and gave me a chance to adjust and then avail myself of the time with the doctor to ask informed questions.

Since that moment, when I was yanked onto the Porch and essentially told to sit down and listen, He has not had to be quite so direct. I have been led to doctors who have provided the care I need. We have been led to career opportunities that put rare caregivers in proximity to which I would not have had access otherwise. God was on the front porch with me during the battles providing resources and sitting with me.

That doesn't mean that there weren't struggles. When I later had the medical emergency on a plane, it was terrifying, but He still provided a haven. I could literally feel myself slipping away, and there was nothing I could do about it. It took all the energy I could muster to lift my hand and write my husband's and parents' names and phone numbers hoping that someone would call them. Yet, in the middle of knowing there was absolutely nothing I could do, the most overwhelming and otherworldly sense of peace came over me that I have ever felt. The only thing I thought about, and the only regret I had, was leaving my family; but I was completely OK that this very well might be the outcome. To emphasize, I didn't think about work, a to do list, any of my possessions – just my family. I let go. I can't explain it except that I was under His wings.

I have never forgotten the flight attendant who gave me oxygen and held my hand across the aisle the entire time it took to divert the plane and land. A second one who had been with me said as I was being carried off the plane, "I am praying for you." The pilot said, "Oh no, she's on her own." The next thing I knew, an airline employee was in the ambulance riding with me to the hospital, and I know the pilot was responsible for ensuring a companion for the journey. She stayed with me the entire time. The airline flew my husband free of charge to my location. At the one stop the flight made, they provided him with an update. By the time he arrived, I had been discharged and accompanied by the same airline employee to a hotel they had arranged. The next day, we were greeted with a special escort to assist us. I wrote letters to the airline, pilots and attendants to thank them for their care and their prayers. The airline sent a thank you note and a blanket, and the crew sent me a card. My husband and I were never alone through the whole ordeal and had a haven wrapped around us the entire time.

We can carry the Porch with us no matter where we go. I was on my way to a college reunion in another state on my own when I got caught about halfway there in a particularly nasty thunderstorm at night. The windshield wipers couldn't keep up with the rain, and I was growing more and more concerned about my safety. Suddenly, my car stopped running in the middle of the interstate. Fortunately, I saw an exit on my right, and there was enough speed left that allowed me to drift around the curve of the ramp to the shoulder. I called 911 for help, and was also able to identify a towing service that would come to take care of things. I let my husband know where I was and what was happening. Meanwhile, the state police pulled up and said, "It's a stormy night. There are accidents, and I can't stay and help you." With that response to protecting and serving, he zoomed off.

Next a car pulled up beside me, and I remember thinking, "Please God, don't let this be an axe murderer." He said, "If this was my wife, I would want someone to help her. I'm going to push you down the ramp so you can drift into the gas station at the bottom on the right." He proceeded to do just that and said he had an errand to run but would be back to make sure that the tow truck showed up. As he drove away, he handed me a card. He was an employee at the local Bible College. I felt the tickle of an angel's wings on my face and knew I was not alone on the porch.

Every day we have the choice of whether we scoot those chairs closer on the porch or hang out in the yard trying to toil away on our own. The haven is well within sight. We deceive ourselves into believing we don't have time, and we take on more than we should when God will provide all the resources we need versus what we think we want. By not watching, listening, and stopping, we fail to discern His voice when He whispers, "Come sit with Me." Mom used to tell me that it was time to come in when the streetlight came on at the end of our driveway. She set the boundary for when I needed to enter the haven of our home as night fell. I never let her get to the point of shouting at me, "Get in here!" Yet, I was perfectly comfortable responding, "I don't want to pick it up!" to the Heavenly Boundary Setter. He was directing me onto the Porch, into the haven, and under His wings, and yet, I fought Him thinking I knew all too well what was good for me. Relax, let go, and rest for a while. Let Him set your front porch boundaries and help you out of crisis mode living.

SOUL SITTIN': LIVING UNDER HIS WING

1. Where are you sitting on the front porch? **Are you even on the front porch?**

2. How are you trusting you as the source and **living on perfectionism?**

3. Recall your stories of when you were **pulled onto the Porch** and provided protection.

   a. What did you learn?
   b. What won't you repeat?

4. When was the **last time you were scared** and had to rely on Him? How did it turn out?

5. Who has shown up and provided a haven for you that was not a relative or a friend that made you wonder where the **source of the help** was coming from?

6. What are you **feeding your mind, body, and spirit** that you are willing to give up to pull closer and live under His wing?

7. How can you **let go of your ego** and know that it's going to be more than OK?

8. How can you **spring into reverence instead of activity** next time you are faced with a crisis?

9. Describe what it **feels like when you are in His haven** and under His wings.

10. What **Porch boundaries** do you need to let Him set for you right now?

SOUL SITTIN' TIPS:

1. Make a list of your stories when you know God was moving in your life. Add to it in the weeks to come as the memories flood back and you can see the connections.

2. Look for the threads in your story of when God was:

    a. Leading you
    b. Protecting you
    c. Correcting you
    d. Delaying gratification
    e. Teaching you
    f. Inspiring you
    g. Pulling your chair closer to the front porch
    h. Yanking you onto the front porch
    i. Letting you run free to learn
    j. Whispering to you to *"Come sit with Me"*

SOUL SITTIN' BLESSING OF REFUGE

***"He will cover you with his feathers, and
under His wings you will find refuge."*** [42]

Help me to scoot my chair a little closer on the porch. Give me the courage to let the arms touch. Let me know that if my chair is a little rickety, has broken spindles, or needs a little paint that You have the resources to give me a bright, shiny, sturdy chair; that there is one that already has my name on it, and it's in the front row on the Porch. Remind me of where You have provided a Haven throughout my life and that it is always there for me. Assist me in accepting the boundaries that You need to place on my life for my safety. Give me the courage to spring into reverence instead of activity when the next crisis turns up. Help me to let go and let You.

---

[42] Psalm 91:4, New International Version

"I have much to write to you, but I do not want to use paper and ink. Instead, I hope to visit you and talk with you face to face, so that our joy may be complete." [43]

FRONT PORCH BLESSINGS

The greatest blessing of all is to live one's life without fear, fully in faith, and therefore with our Heavenly and earthly front porches always in deep connection. It would be wonderful if life was as simple as plugging in a cord, living with our batteries fully charged and our interactions on point every day. We're complicated creatures, and we live in a world in which complete communication has been reduced to emoticons, a hundred and forty characters, and texts. While at times, they can be very effective tools; fully expressive they are not. Who would want to miss the joy and surprise on a child's face when they take their first

---

[43] 2 John 1: 12, New International Version

steps and have it replaced with only hearing the cry of glee over the phone? What is missed in the body language, the facial expressions, and the interactions with other people goes almost beyond description. Being in the moment with people adds rich dimensions to our experience. If talking face to face creates joy in relationships with human beings, how much more is our joy magnified when sitting on the Porch with Jesus in prayer? What caliber of blessings are we willing to forego?

Nothing could be truer than our efforts to be fully present for the blessings of front Porch connections. My Dad taught me "your life is a prayer." It took me quite a while to process the depth of that declaration. How I am to *be* is always in prayer. "Pray without ceasing."[44] Always *be* in conversation with God. This requires actively doing as well, which means that I'm always supposed to have my earthly and Heavenly front porches connected. I'm supposed to pull up my chair close and "sit for a spell." By living my life in this fashion, I am actively creating a connection through which both assignments and blessings can flow. I am saying, "Yes" to the fullest life possible designed specifically for me. The quality of my "yes" also impacts every person I come into contact with and whether they receive the most complete blessing that my presence can bring. It affects how much light radiates to them through me.

What are some of the outcomes of making this choice to stand in the space of assignment and blessing? Maybe I could stop living in nervousness and "have to's" before whatever is coming up next. I've had to work on the amnesia that sometimes strikes when it comes to "We are God's workmanship, created in Christ Jesus to do good

---

[44] 1st Thessalonians 5:17, English Standard Version

works, which God prepared in advance for us to do."[45] Whether it is a speech, a coaching session, a consultation, board facilitation, or just a conversation; if I gain the skills, prepare, and do the work, I don't have to be enough. He'll be enough if it's His assignment. "I can do all things through Christ, who strengthens me."[46]

I used to prepare well for speaking engagements, practice, and sometimes I'd lose sleep the night before. I would be so concerned that I would make myself look stupid, not deliver for the audience, or let down someone who had entrusted me to deliver for them. Then, one day I remembered. Yes, I confess I remembered to start praying prior to the phone call, the meeting, the speaking engagement, the coaching session, or writing. I would acknowledge that I didn't know what others needed to hear or what the best outcome would be but that He did. I didn't have the language for it then, but I was connecting my front porches. Invariably, I would hear words coming out of my mouth that I had absolutely no idea were going to be there or content for publications would be written born out of nothing, the equivalent of mastering the artist's dreaded blank canvas. Sometimes, my tone, the methods, or my silence were used as strong tools in key moments. If you had asked me before how I was going to manage something, I would have provided a completely different answer or none at all. These experiences allowed me to trust "Do not be anxious about anything, but in every situation, by prayer and petition, with thanksgiving, present your requests to God."[47]

Another benefit and blessing of living fully in faith is the return of severed connections to our lives at just the right moment. Years ago,

---

[45] Ephesians 2:10, New International Version
[46] Philippians 4:13, New King James Version, copyright 1982 by Thomas Nelson, Inc.
[47] Philippians 4:6, New International Version

a friend wrote a letter that I chose to take exception to after feeling as though I had made a particular effort to nurture this long distance relationship. The rules of friendship from my perspective kept changing. Not particularly adept at resolving conflict at this stage in my life, I walked away from the friendship without dealing with the issues. Over a couple of decades, it gnawed at me. I never felt good about how we parted. Certainly, there were maturity issues on both parts that played into the circumstances, and both parties felt wounded.

I give all credit to my friend who reached out to me years later to mend the relationship. I am thankful that I responded in a positive way. Over one dinner, with willingness to understand where the other had been at that moment in time, we quickly handled what we should have dealt with years before with love and forgiveness. That's the sad part; that while we lived far away, we had forfeited the support and friendship we could have been to each other had we stayed connected. God worked to bring two stubborn women of faith back together just before He knew that we would be living in the same area again. She was courageous to reach out, and as a result, we reconnected our front porches because of God's love through us. Had either of us chosen to ignore the gnawing or acted out of fear of rejection, we would have missed the blessings we have enjoyed since.

Of course, living in faith also requires you to answer the calling and live fully without fear in service to your purpose. For me, it included faith to create a business, write this book, and step away from the illusion of an employer paycheck as the source for my well-being and comfort. The false belief was that the source of that paycheck was something that I was creating or doing on a regular basis instead of Him. It also encompassed the willingness to be open daily to new assignments that were not apparent yet and to trust that talent and gifts would be used in His time, not mine, which would be the source of future provision. It required the recognition that callings can alter over time or be used in different ways and with new audiences. I came across this Neale Donald Walsch quote that convicted me to the core.

> "Money is not the issue. Having the courage to give your highest gift is the issue. There is no security in doing something for a living when you are dying inside while doing it. That is taking care of the body at the expense of the soul. And a withering soul cannot help but produce a withering body. So do not think you are "taking care of yourself" by killing your spirit to keep your body alive. How long will you put off what you are dying to do?"[48]

A client had struggled with similar issues having built a business that was providing financial security to the family and at the same time required divesting of some interests no longer perceived to be in line with their core values. There was also a yearning to do other things in service with his life. The fear was losing the ability to provide, to be the protector, and to have long-term comfort for the future. Those for whom he was providing had already spoken words of freedom and released him from any real or perceived commitments. He now knew the full freedom of the earthly front porch coupled with God's freedom in securing his path in life. In other words, there were no excuses not to answer the call. He also knew the restlessness to risk it all, be obedient, and to act in faith without fear. During the time this occurred with the client, I went for my prayer walk and took this photo of the sign I saw outside a

---

[48] Neale Donald Walsch, facebook.com, Timeline Photos, July 11, 2014

nearby church. I emailed it to him as he left for a mission trip as a bon voyage present from God.

This occurred as I wrestled with my own fear of answering the next phase of my calling. Nothing like having a mirror held up to you on the porch. New people were showing up encouraging me to write, and clients were coming on board from a variety of places. I was trying to pull my chair up close to see whether my ego was leading me, whether I was being tempted not to finish the last calling, or whether I was actually late and should have answered the new calling a while ago. Yes, sometimes, handwriting on the wall would be welcomed.[49]

And then, twice in two weeks, people who had no idea what I was going through prayed for me to know that God had more planned for me than I could ever imagine and used those same words. One of them said God had known me before I was here, hence the first Bible verse under the photo in Chapter One of this book. The first person to utter those words was during the "Be Still" themed retreat during the self-imposed sabbatical. At the end of the day, we were offered the opportunity to receive a blessing. I had never experienced that other than the benediction at the end of a Sunday service, so I was curious and open.

---

[49] Daniel 5:5, New International Version

We sat facing each other on two rockers after night had fallen, just as the photo shows at the opening of this chapter. As this perfect stranger, who had nothing to gain and who knew nothing about me, prayed for me, she reminded me of my Source, of His care, of my purpose, and of the utter trust I could have in what was already set on the table for me. All I had to do was to be present in faith releasing all fear.

As the tears flowed down my face while she prayed, I wondered how on earth she could possibly have reached into my soul and known where I was, what I was struggling with, and what needed to be interceded for on my behalf? How did she know that I needed the reassurance that the plan was already written, to just step out on faith? Of course, now I know that she was connecting my front porches for me. Even though I had gone to the mountain the day before and heard, "Don't leave in the middle of the storm. It's the most dangerous time for you," I also needed to know that the storm would end and that what was coming was going to be far more than I could ever design, dream, or plan. Just as the opportunity to study abroad, travel the world, and lead large organizations was nothing I could ever have dreamed up or figured out how to make happen from the venue of my tiny bedroom in a small town in Virginia, there was more to come. Even sharing with you via this book takes these very personal experiences to an audience beyond any expectations I would have had. You don't have to design on your own. My stories, questions, and prayers are only the catalyst for you to sit for a spell, remember your stories and connect your front porches knowing that you can do so in co-creation and without fear.

When you let go, you operate from a completely different place. You can literally feel the barriers being removed, because you don't have to figure out how to scale them, go around them, or climb over them anymore. That does not mean you do not have to put effort in. It does mean that in being available and showing up, you aren't going it on your own. That is freeing. It connects you to resources that you would not be able to avail yourself of otherwise. It removes the blockages to live in full truth and peace. It has happened to me in quite simple and yet dramatic ways. It went from a scarcity mindset to these are not my resources. He will provide. God knows what we need (not want), and we can contribute charitably to others free from worry of whether we may need something in the future. No more worrying about what is coming. Get on with taking care of others, and do what we are called to do.

The blessings of the front Porch call us to plan for our assignments and yet pay attention. As you are honed and refocused from what you anticipate occurring, know that there is a reason. Follow through on the adjustment that presents itself. Notice when that thing you thought was so important doesn't wind up needing to get done at all or winds up not needing to happen for a few more days. There are reasons and order for how things occur that you are not controlling and don't need to control. Over time, you will get better at discerning whether you are trying to make something happen yourself and hiding any personal motives, even from yourself, or whether you are trusting that it's going to get done in "the fullness of time."[50] As you live your life as a prayer, complete each phase and assignment of your calling while living in the space of receiving blessings in freedom.

---

[50] Galatians 4:4-5, English Standard Version

SOUL SITTIN': BEING WITHOUT FEAR IN FREEDOM THROUGH FAITH

1. **Replacing fear with faith** requires you to be in relationship with something. With whom are you in relationship?

2. What is the **source of your faith**?

3. How is your **life a prayer**?

4. Are you **going to the Porch before or after** you set out on your assignment?

5. Whose front porch have you not been on lately out of fear of rejection, pride, neglect, or past experiences that you need to reconnect with? Are you willing to shackle fear and commit to being the first one to **reach out in obedience and courage** to them?

6. Are you behind the glass like an animal in a zoo, observing the other side with **inertia or part of God's re-creation**? What will it take for you to **release yourself from the cage of fear**?

7. Are you **clinging to comfort** versus clinging to Him?

8. What is being **asked of you** that creates a blessing for others?

9. What do you **gain short term and long term** by staying where you are versus stepping out on faith?

10. What **blessings are you missing out on** as you restrain yourself from living fully and freely without fear?

SOUL SITTIN' TIPS:

1. Examine honestly what you are "dying to do."[51] Are you daily invested in work and assignments that you know are fulfilling a calling? If not, what steps do you need to take:

   a. To admit any role money may be playing in keeping you tied to your present state?

   b. To make peace with any loss of title or stature in your community or profession?

   c. To receive the support of those who will be affected when you make this change?

   d. To acknowledge your fears about not being in control and having the answers for how it will happen?

2. Create a plan that outlines all of the issues that you believe need to be handled in order to turn over what you are "dying to do"[52] to God, and ask Him for peace to let go of these areas and assistance in dealing with each item. Watch to see how quickly movement occurs, all the while praying for His will to be revealed and for His blessing.

---

[51] Neale Donald Walsch, facebook.com, Timeline Photos, July 11, 2014
[52] Neale Donald Walsch, Facebook.com, Time Line Photos, July 11, 2014

SOUL SITTIN': BLESSING FOR YOUR WORK

"But whoever looks intently into the perfect law
that gives freedom, and continues in it – not
forgetting what they have heard, but doing it
– they will be blessed in what they do."[53]

I step into the space of receiving your assignments and blessing for my work. My prayer is to live my life as a prayer, to come to you at the beginning of the work and not as a second thought. I claim freedom for my life as I undertake the assignments that you have for me without fear. I pray that I will experience you shining through my soul from the Porch in such a way that my work is a blessing to others. Help me to always see the real work and to play my part fully by doing my homework in order to be a talented vessel that can be used to the fullest. Prepare me to be open to your blessings so you can fill me up, allowing me to live completely in faith without fear. Teach me to learn how to receive graciously, and in turn, to reciprocate to those whom you place in my path.

---

[53] James 1:25, New International Version

*"My soul thirsts for God, for the living God.
When can I go and meet with God?"*[54]

DECORATING THE FRONT PORCH
FOR A ROYAL VISIT

A couple of summers ago, I rose early to indulge in being an Anglophile.
Living in England, visiting often, and being married to a Yorkshireman
have made me a lover of all things British. On this particular morning,
an entire nation had dressed itself up to celebrate the Jubilee of the
Queen - sixty years on a throne, not quite as long as Victoria, but
a significant milestone deserving of recognition and unlikely to be
repeated in the next three generations of subsequent kings in line to the
throne. Street parties, face painting, wild attire, special food, and elated
mobs of happy citizens could be found from one end of the islands to the
other, accompanied by festivities in the Commonwealth nations around

---

[54] Psalm 42:2, New International Version

the world. Work was paused while a tribute fitting her service was paid to a woman who had dedicated her life to others, whose family came second, whose relatives paid the price for duty, and who believed her calling was from God. She had publicly demonstrated this through her prohibition of showing the anointing portion of the first ever televised broadcast of a Coronation Service. Sixty years later, the Thames was a parking lot as a procession of water joyriders escorted the royal family on their trip through London, acknowledging her humility and the debt that could never be repaid.

Millennia before, a small town saw streets bursting with jubilant followers, waving palm branches as a humble carpenter and itinerant Rabbi in a robe and sandals rode on a donkey surrounded by those He had served. Food had been multiplied. The ill had regained their strength. The distressed had found peace. The yearning had known solace. A presence unknown before or since, He was identified and recognized as their Servant and yet was worthy of their following. The debt that knows no repayment had yet to be paid, but the streets were dense with shouts of praise and clothed in a royal suit of palms.

We know when we are in the presence of what is worthy of honor. In an instant, we spot it in a YouTube video as tears run down our face as families welcome soldiers home from war. The movie of the year moves us with unselfishness, feats of recovery, or lives of dedication. The hush falls in a universal knowing when we come face to face with a Gandhi, Mother Theresa or Nelson Mandela, and we know that their strength is not of this world. They have submitted to something much greater than themselves. They are being led, directed, and sustained, and they know it is not by them but through them. They have said, "Yes" to the long journey not to immediate gratification. They are aware it's not a personal mission but a grand vision upon which the mantle of responsibility has been placed. They know that it is not necessarily a safe undertaking, but it is the fulfillment of their lifetime for which they were assigned. They are not great themselves, but they have been faithful to the ask put on their soul.

To be ready to take on our assignment, we must prepare for a royal visit. Our ego must be subservient to the journey we are to be sent on. We don't leave on the trip without having experienced the royal visit, without packing appropriately, and without staying in touch with the Guide who goes before us. We can choose not to take these steps, and there are consequences for doing so.

Before Moses led his people, he had a royal visit in the form of a burning bush. He wasn't so sure about the assignment and had to overcome stuttering in order to speak to masses of followers. He even queried God about the task, "Are you sure about this God? Are you certain you've got the right person here? I'm not so good at the speaking part. Where is it that we're going again?" Even someone who was having direct interactions with God in ways that are hard for us to conceive today had the arrogance to question God's ability to do whatever God wanted accomplished. Moses even had to be reminded to take his shoes off when standing on holy ground.

Moses is such a beautiful example of our humanity and the stumbling around we do in our lives. We have momentary, and sometimes lengthy, phases of amnesia of the Porch, of whom we serve, and that we're not here for our own pointless joyride. Imagine having the good fortune of being saved from slaughter when your Mother puts you in a basket on the water, and of all people, Pharaoh's sister finds you and decides to become your new mom. You are raised in the luxury of Egypt with your birth mother as a servant nearby to protect you and to keep connecting you to the Porch, guarding your heart from a competing culture.

When royal visits have become your daily porch experience, you then find out who you really are and learn that there is another Porch with which you have a direct connection. Sometimes He is expecting something pretty dramatic from you and starts showing up on your porch making demands about what you are supposed to do with your life. He's got you after you commit a sin like murder and still chases after you in self-imposed exile as He did Moses. The royal visits don't stop, and suddenly, you're wandering around in a desert on the way to a new home of which you have no conception. Your royal visits have led you to utter submission and stepping out on faith with no way to Google what the real estate is going to look like, who your enemies might be along the way, what you should put in your suitcase, or even how long you're going to be away.

Today, we whine when we don't live in a house as large as our neighbor's, when our car isn't the latest model, when our colleague gets the promotion, or when our children don't get into the university of highest reputation. We forget that there is a journey already mapped out for us, and that often times, what we yearn for is something from which we need protection. We can't see that if we were in a particular place at that specific time that there are connections that would take us off the path and put us in danger. We don't know that there would be experiences that would create desires that are unhealthy for us or people who would gladly prevent us from fulfilling our role.

For example, while many today wrestle with the biblical roles of husbands and wives, in our partnership my husband has the "no" vote. Before this puts off thousands of women, let me explain that we didn't have "obey" in our vows and offer some clarification about what I mean. Just as there is a feminine intuition or gut instinct that has been scientifically validated and a presence of God I have learned to rely upon, which my husband has learned to trust, I also became aware of a different and equally valid knowing that my husband has in his capabilities. In our marriage, he is chief cheerleader, healthy enabler, rock strong supporter, caregiver, and believer in me. Three times, he gave up major career opportunities to, as he would say, "follow my star." He has declared that his reason for being is to look after me and sees me as his assignment. This is not suffocating but freeing, as he has helped me to unfold my wings, created a platform of confidence, and been unselfish in the significant time away from our home that my assignments have required of me.

He has the ability to see into a situation, cut to the core, and spot danger, including people whose intent is questionable. In almost thirty years, he has used his "no" twice. The first instance had to do with my safety. He was right. The second time required a longer revealing of the decision's wisdom, and he was right again. He'll laugh and say that the reason he still has a "no" vote is because he has batted 1000! Neither of these were instances of "I'm the man, or I'm your husband, and I say no." These experiences both involved recognition on my part that he was tuned into something I could not see. I respected his abilities and knew in each case that following his lead was the right thing to do, even though in the second scenario, I could not see clearly at the time to what he was pointing. However, he saw how our journey would unfold and served as protector so that we did not get off course from the ultimate plan or wander through a desert. He kept us true to the course corrections needed from our royal visits.

Experiencing a royal visit can come without warning, and it can also come by invitation. The more we connect our front porches, sit down, and wait for His arrival, the more frequently He is going to show up. Our job is to decorate our front porch for the visit. It includes taking the steps that we've been outlining together on this journey so far. If our front porch is all junked up with stuff, there is no room for Him to sit down. If we don't even have a chair for Him, I'm sure He would stand for us, but what are we saying to Him? "I don't have time for you. There is a place in my life for everything but you. I kept the most beautiful plants inside the house for me to look at, so there is nothing left to brighten up the area in which we're going to spend our time together on the porch. Beauty is for me to hoard, not for us to share. I can't be bothered to fix the floorboards so that you don't fall over. You're God, what does my effort matter?" If we don't show up ourselves having done the work and sought His presence and will for our journey, why should He? We need to remember to take the cover off His chair.

Preparation for a royal visit should be highlighted like a sixty-year Jubilee celebration. We should pause everything else that we are doing to honor the One whose debt cannot be repaid. Our hearts should be swept in all chambers so that nothing remains but open space for love to fill us up. Our minds should be full of the stories of His presence through our life. Our souls should be poised to recognize the moment of arrival as the Heavenly Front Porch touches our front porch. Our bodies should be fully on the porch, not on the grass with one foot on the first step of the porch, not leaning against the post easily able to run down the steps off the porch, but in the chair expectantly waiting to feel His guiding hand on the back of our chair as He sits down next to us. We don't have to wait for sixty years to pass. We don't have to hope that a gilded invitation to the ball arrives in the mail. We can have a royal visit every moment of every day if we will but prepare and show up ourselves. Our life can be a prayer.[55]

---

[55] Rev. Charles Spraker, father of the author.

SOUL SITTIN': RECOGNIZING & ACKNOWLEDGING THE HEAVENLY FRONT PORCH

1. When was your **last royal visit,** and what was your experience?

2. What royal visits stand out in your life as **significant to your journey?**

3. If you've never had a royal visit, are you **open to receiving a Visitor?**

4. What do you need to do to **decorate** your front porch to receive a royal visit?

5. What do you need to **sweep out from your heart?**

6. What are you clinging to that could be **putting you in danger?**

7. Where are you on your earthly front porch? Do you need to **shift positions?**

8. What can you point to that indicates you are now **ready for a Royal Visit?**

9. What can you demonstrate that confirms your **readiness for the next assignment?**

10. If there are any **changes you need to make,** note them here.

SOUL SITTIN' TIPS:

1. When the Queen of Sheba visited Solomon, she came because of the reports of his wisdom, wealth, fame, and relationship to the Lord. After her royal visit, "King Solomon gave the queen of Sheba all she desired and asked for, besides what he had given her out of his royal bounty."[56] In this royal visit, she recognized the God of Abraham. "Praise be to the Lord your God, who has delighted in you and placed you on the throne of Israel. Because of the Lord's eternal love for Israel, he has made you king to maintain justice and righteousness."[57] Even royalty visiting royalty acknowledged the Source of their power, riches, and wisdom, giving tribute to the position they held in society.

2. Think about what you have achieved in life to date whether it is an education, a family, surviving trauma, tackling health challenges, career moves, getting out of debt, learning to live with difficult people, or finding peace in the middle of chaos. Visit your own stories and see where the royal visits were

---

[56] 1 Kings 10:13, New International Version
[57] 1 Kings 10:9, New International Version

occurring throughout. Acknowledge where you left the path of the journey and the consequences. See where provision or protection was made for you even when you were not aware of the visits.

3. Allow yourself to realize that when the sun comes up tomorrow, you're on a journey. Decide whether you are going to offer a royal invitation. Write down the invitation and word it fit for your Lord. Set a date and time, describe the event, and ask specifically for a Royal Visit. Sit down on the porch tomorrow and meet your Guest.

SOUL SITTIN' BLESSING FIT FOR A KING

"So be content with who you are, and don't put on airs. God's strong hand is on you; he'll promote you at the right time." [58]

With excitement, anticipation, and reverence, I take my seat on the front porch waiting for your Porch to dock. My mind is clear. My heart is open. My body is present. My soul is committed to sitting here with You. I come to You waiting for my next assignment and knowing that You created good works for me to do here. [59] I recognize that what I may want and what You may have for me may be two completely different things. I know that what I want may be based on the earthly definitions of success. I ask for Your strength to give me peace about the assignments You have for me and to take pride in their execution. I request the blessing of knowing that I am contributing to Your Kingdom in the way that You see fit, using the talents and gifts You gave me in combination with my willingness to be Your servant. I am ready for a Royal Visit.

---

[58] 1 Peter 5: 6, The Bible in Contemporary Language, copyright 2002 by Eugene Peterson
[59] Ephesians 2:10, New International Version

"And this is love: that we walk in
obedience to his commands." [60]

STAYING ON THE FRONT PORCH

We've talked about coming home to the front porch, the safety of the front porch, and the communion of the front porches, but we haven't discussed how hard it is sometimes to simply stay on the front porch and wait. Yes, this is the obedience chapter. Just like a tantrum by our own child, we protest and disobey, because we don't want to; we're tired; and we think we know better.

---

[60] 2 John: 1:6, New International Version

Difficulty waiting can be born from a number of pregnant sources. We may be incredibly excited about having discovered a new skill set, so we desperately search for places to practice it, not fully considering the appropriateness of our choices. We may have made a new connection that seems to be right in the wheelhouse of our professional needs, but without testing it, the timing could be completely wrong. We may meet someone who seems to have arrived to help us with a particularly challenging situation. Without further verification, they turn out to be less than a blessing and more of a distraction leading to unnecessary chaos.

"Wait for the Lord"[61] may very well be one of the most difficult commands we receive, whether by the seasoned follower or the new traveler on the journey. Pulling up your chair on the front porch, sitting down, and staying put when the ice tea has run out, the sandwich is gone, the dog is asleep, all your friends have gone home, the music has stopped, and you can't quite feel the calming touch on the back of your chair, causes us to squirm.

When we feel alone, get anxious, and aren't recipients of an immediate response, it's all we can do not to start raising ourselves up out of the chair on the porch. If we obey the hand that pushes us back down into the chair and stay on the porch, remaining vigilant, favor arrives in the form of protection, guidance, and peace. When we keep fighting it and take solo action, we find ourselves in chaos, out of timing, and clamoring to get back on the front porch.

My story on waiting for the Lord covers a span of about 15 years. After I received the offer to lead the international organization following the

---

[61] Psalm 27:14, New International Version

chronic illness diagnosis, I worked for them for about six years. We made significant strides in helping them to transition into a new era, but eventually, I found myself getting restless, though I did nothing to address it. We lived in a part of the country that my husband was really enjoying, had a lovely home, and terrific friends. I traveled frequently, had wonderful colleagues nationally and internationally, earned my profession's certification, and contributed to my profession as a volunteer. It sounds like a great life. However, I've learned through experience that when that particular restless feeling presents itself, it is usually God preparing me for the next assignment. He creates a level of dissatisfaction that I can't quite put my finger on and generates openness for me to consider and desire a change.

One day, my phone rang, and a headhunter said, "Your name is at the top of the list." I asked him to what list he was referring and learned that there was a national trade association position open in the northeast of the U.S. I could have immediately responded that we had no desire to live in the frozen north, but I knew that I needed to listen to this opportunity. Women rarely had the chance to run a national trade association at that time. I knew that if it got around the headhunters that I had turned this down when my "name was at the top of the list," it could have future career ramifications.

To make a long story short, every door opened and all the signs pointed that this was where we were supposed to be. My husband, who would not be excited about the location, was made ready to accept this change too. He told me much later that as soon as we got the call, he knew we were moving. To be clear about the lengths to which he was also being prepared, he has no desire to experience winter in any of its forms. He made good on the promise he volunteered to me upon our marriage that we would follow my star at a time when I had no clue in what universe my star was even located. Three times, significant career opportunities presented themselves to both of us at the same time, and three times, my husband said, "We're not having a conversation about this. We're going where the doors are opening for you."

This position turned out to be an absolutely magical fit. I loved the people. My husband enjoyed their company. I traveled nationally and internationally, spoke, consulted for related organizations to help raise all boats, and worked with a brilliant team of staff and board members who created new programs. Together, we took the organization to a completely different level of supporting the members and transformed an industry as we had set out to do. It was a privilege and an honor to serve with them.

That being said, there were a few bumps in the road early on as people jostled through change, and I checked out a Plan B just in case. In this nosing around, I was picked as one of the top candidates for an enormous and high profile Washington, D.C. organization. The interview process was the most intense I have ever experienced with the Search Committee Chair flying up to meet me first, a series of essays to be written, a video to be created responding to another set of questions, an interview by Committee, and then a large VIP reception. I was asked to lead the organization and was beyond excited to have been chosen. This was a career defining moment.

However, just as the selection process was cumbersome so were the contract negotiations. As I continued down this path, I started hearing, "Who is going to shepherd these people if you leave?" The first time I heard this, I thought, "Whhaaattt????" It was that same voice from

"PICK IT UP!!" about ten years before. I remember thinking, "Really? This is an amazing opportunity that anyone would be thrilled to have offered during a career and to have on a resume. I've been through this whole process and been selected for this incredible position. My career path has prepared me for this, and now, You're asking me not to go?" So I kept pressing forward. Yes, I was off the front porch now, heading down a path on my own.

As the contract process unfolded, I realized that it was revealing an environment they intended to keep in place, which would prohibit them from receiving from me what they had indicated they were so excited to purchase. My skill set, expertise, and experience would be thwarted. I called my Dad for advice, and he gave me great counsel on how to extract in the next conversation indications of whether or not they were open to alternative ways of operating that would in fact result in the outcomes they were seeking by hiring me.

As I walked further away from the front porch, I kept hearing repeatedly, "Who is going to shepherd these people if you leave?" Knowing that I did not converse with myself using phraseology like that, I knew this was definitely not in my head. It was recognizably that same voice again. As much as I was exhausted from the process that resulted in being offered this job, and very proud of being chosen - yes, pride reared its head, the next phone call divulged the truth. While they absolutely wanted me, they also absolutely could not have what they wanted with the steadfast decision to keep the current environment. I came back to the front porch, put my ego in a box, and declined the position. The voice was silenced, and I went on to spend almost eleven supremely happy years at the organization that had brought me to the northeast.

Into the midst of this wonderful synergy of people, mission, and calling, the phone rang with a life-altering message. My father announced that he had Stage IV chronic lymphocytic leukemia. After a weekend on the Internet, I realized that the state of affairs was dire and the likelihood of my Dad surviving the summer was slim. With my mother journeying down the path of Alzheimer's as her mother and grandfather before had trod, I knew where this roadmap led. With an older husband who had presented with significant heart disease two years earlier, as his father had, I also knew that my role ahead had just been redefined as caregiver for an undetermined number of years.

There are plenty of mistakes I have made in my life, both from things done and undone, that I strive not to repeat. With more years of noticing behind me, I also work to avoid errors by trying to be a better navigator in advance. The one thing I was not going to do was to have regrets about not honoring my father and mother[62] or not being present for the three people I loved most in the world as they went through their final journeys. That meant, I could not fulfill this new role from where I was presently living, nor could I stay in a job I loved in a location that I really enjoyed with a church that had become a haven.

Let's take a side journey for a moment and talk about preparation. On the one hand, it is accurate to paint the picture of my circumstances at the time as very happy. On the other hand, and with hindsight, I can see the groundwork being laid to have me ready to go. A year before Dad's call, I had injured a knee that took a year to heal with physical therapy. Every time I got on a plane, which was often, I was hurting myself somehow on the trip. Physically, I was tired. I was coincidentally

---

[62] Exodus 20:12, New International Version

visiting the city we would be relocated to more often for meetings, was reconnecting with old friends there, making new friends, and had even checked out a local seminary that I was interested in attending.

When my husband got sick, I started thinking about the life I would one day lead on my own. Not knowing whether it was sooner or later, I started trying on lives to see what I liked and what I was good at becoming a Certified Master Coach, teaching in a Master's program, and starting my own company for executive coaching, board and leadership development, speaking and facilitation, and consulting. Because of the need to preserve energy, I had fallen into the habit of participating in church via Sunday broadcasts, until one day I heard, "How long are you going to wait?" Two years before my Dad's call, I went to the church near my home that became a sanctuary to me of friends and support, particularly after my Dad's news. I was being cared for in advance and prepared for life as it would unfold in the years to come.

I flew to my hometown and went to Dad's chemo appointment the next month. Along with praying for his recovery, I started praying intensely to God, "How on earth do you expect me to manage this from here?" There was no way that I could perform the job I had, travel constantly, and be at my parents' side through what I expected to be a downhill journey. Meanwhile, my Dad completed his treatment over a period of months and responded well. However, his form of leukemia hides and can come back at any time. We couldn't claim victory and then go back to life as normal. Life as normal was who knows what's next all the time? I continued praying. I had the church praying. Heaven's gates were being bombarded with "What now?" I started getting "Wait for the Lord." There was that voice again. I responded, "You *know* I'm not very good with waiting. I've got more patience than I used to have according to my husband, but you *know* this is not one of my strong suits." Staying seated on that front porch was one of the hardest things I've ever done, particularly in those circumstances.

One day, I went to the computer and thought, "I'm just going to stick my toe in the water and see what's out there." The very first job at the top of the list was in my alma mater's city nine hundred miles away. I literally pushed back in the chair and felt a knowing that if I applied, we were going. This was the city my husband and I had married in, a place with built-in friends and a support system for the next phase of life. The location had a climate that was agreeable to my husband and a proximity to my parents that would allow us to either visit easier or move them closer, depending on what happened. I went downstairs and said to him, "There's this job in…" He responded, "What are you doing down here then?" Receiving his immediate blessing, I later learned that he too thought, "We're moving."

Had I not waited for the Lord, the answers to all of my prayers that He had been preparing for all four of us would not have been available as I would have pushed on to other options of my own identification that would have led us elsewhere. From the moment of application, I knew this was a result of me staying put on the front porch. During the second call with the headhunter, I shared how much it would mean to return and give back to a community that had contributed to my development. I pointed out that one of my mentors there was like a second father to me, and I talked about coming back to visit during his final illness and how much he meant to me as President of my alma mater. The phone went silent, and I thought, "Oh dear, I've shared too much too soon." The headhunter responded, "Cynthia, my father was his doctor." I felt as though my mentor had tapped me on the shoulder and said, "We've got this covered for you, girl. It's all going to be fine." In that moment, the relief I felt sitting on the front porch was immense. I knew that this was God calling me to the next assignment. I didn't miss it, because I had stayed on the front porch. I was a pest, but I was on the front porch.

I was offered the position, and we moved. My Dad has survived to date, seven years past his diagnosis, and is able to care for my Mom. They moved into a continuous care community that has given them a peace of mind and all four of us the gift of time due to its proximity. The identification and quality of the community is another story of blessing. My husband is in the care of great doctors who are helping him to live as long a life as possible. His plan handled everything and was designed in a way that I never could have even remotely created.

There is a footnote to be shared about behavior on the front porch. This was about a calling to obedience, putting family first, and accepting a phase that redirected my career away from running national or international organizations. I did have to identify the blessing in the form in which it arrived and recognize this was not all about me. I had started my career as the number two at a national organization and had worked and travelled as the CEO of a national or international organization ever since. My new responsibilities were not on this same scale and yet were a perfect fit for my skill set and experience. Somewhere along the line, I was so consumed by my needs that it had passed me by that He just might want something from me too.

I had stayed on the front porch. I had been obedient. I had done the work, but the blindness of my soul to doing His work after my problems got handled was embarrassing. At the point of my recognition and apology,

I placed on my desk the following scripture, which has remained there ever since.

> *"Whatever you do, do your work heartily, as*
> *for the Lord rather than for men."*[63]

When I find myself challenged, I look down and say to myself, "Remember who your Boss is and why you're doing this work." As I've contemplated the next phase of my life, I have continued to stay on the porch and seek His will, remembering to wait for the calling – His assignment in His time.

---

[63] Colossians 3:23, New American Standard Bible

SOUL SITTIN': WAITING FOR THE CALL

1. When was the last time you have done something for your family, friends, church, charity, or your work that you **knew was a calling**?

2. Think back through your life and record for yourself each time you have experienced a calling. Note **how you felt** in the moment, what you chose to do, and how you felt after your choices were made.

3. What is your **greatest regret** related to a calling? Did you not answer? Were you impatient? Did you leave the front porch?

4. Have your **forgiven yourself**? If not, do some soul sittin' and determine what you can do to rectify the matter, if it's possible now. If not, do some more soul sittin', and treat yourself as you would someone who was seeking your forgiveness. If you need to ask for Divine forgiveness as well, take some more time, and seek His comfort.

5. Are you hearing a calling on your life now? If so, where are you in **responding to it**? If you are pausing or ignoring it, identify for yourself why you are hesitating. Consider what you might be missing by not stepping into the role that is waiting for you.

6. If you believe that you have never felt a calling on your life, go through these four steps: **"Find your passion, know your values, pray for guidance, and live your dream."** When you wait patiently on the front porch, your dream will be His dream and the alignment will fulfill you in a way that you could not create. That does not mean there won't be difficult times. It does mean that you have to remember the identity of your Boss.

SOUL SITTIN' TIPS:

1. When you start practicing staying on the porch, start with simply sitting there. Clear your mind, stop any activity, and just simply *be* on the porch. Whether you are actually sitting on a porch or in the special place you have set aside in your home, your backyard, or the park, just be still.

2. Identify all of the things that you would like to have happen next in your life. Save them in notes on your iPad, or write them in your journal. Acknowledge that these are your dreams.

3. Note where your ego is attached to each of those dreams. Which ones bring you title, stature, or money, fill a void in you, or make you somehow feel better? Recognize that if you are granted your dream, it is only in your best interests if you use it to leverage good and Divine will, not to feed your ego.

4. Ask yourself if you are wedded to what you wrote, and be really honest about your willingness to let go if you are called upon to do something completely different.

5. Test your patience capacity. When you find yourself itching to leave the front porch, make yourself stay another five minutes, 10 minutes, 30 minutes, or an hour with nothing changing.

6. Take notice of your capacity to be at peace when you hear nothing or when you don't receive the answer you were expecting.

SOUL SITTIN' BLESSING OF PATIENCE FOR THE JOURNEY

"Wait for the Lord; be strong and take heart and wait for the Lord."[64]

I want to step off the front porch so badly. I have inched my chair closer and closer to the steps. I have taken my shoes off, and one toe is hanging onto the top step. Help me to stay in the chair, to pull my toe back, and to put my shoes on. I know that Your timing is the right timing, and I know You know better than me. Help me to see the work that You are calling me to and to rejoice that when I am doing that work, it is what You had already identified for me to complete even before I arrived here.

Remind me that it's not about me, even though I run my thoughts and plans through that filter long before I remember to stop and put my ego in a box. Give me the strength to simply sit and rock for a while on the porch while You get everything sorted out. Nudge me when I'm supposed to take action. Help me not to make excuses for my actions when I try to justify getting ahead of You and am really just being impatient.

---

[64] Psalm 27:14, New International Version

"Trust in the Lord with all your heart and lean not to your own understanding. In all your ways submit to Him, and He will make your paths straight."[65]

FRONT PORCH ARCHITECTURE

Though there are plenty of detractors to preacher's kid status, one of the benefits is learning early on about the gulf that exists between a fallible human-run institution and a relationship with God that grows into a sturdy faith. Even before you have the words, it doesn't take long to observe and grasp the concept that judging God, His plan, or even His very existence, based on what you see of human works aren't even related. Without the benefits of these early observations, taking the leap over these blockages to take your seat on the front porch can be trying. It often involves a journey over a period of time with an internal engine that sputters and a compass that seems to have forgotten the location of true north. It's why selecting those you allow onto your porch must be done with wisdom and

---

[65] Proverbs 3: 5-6, New International Version

discernment. They will either gently slide your chair little by little off the porch, or help you install steel brackets that weld it to the floorboards.

One of my observations over the years is that we teach the ritual of religion, in other words "the doing" of it, very effectively. We don't do such a great job of learning how to knit the relationship without dropping stitches. We're missing the choreography of how to hear Him, see His work, identify His presence, and follow the threads of our own story in tandem with Him. We show up to church, say grace, learn the Lord's prayer, make offerings, take Communion, give to the poor; and yet even in the writing of this, it sounds like a checklist of "doing." There is nothing wrong with the actions in this roster of appropriate behavior, and in fact, all are part of a practice. Admittedly, even staying in alignment with completing this list can be difficult at times, as we figure out how to integrate life between the Heavenly and earthly front porches.

Ritual certainly has its place, as does tradition. Repetition reminds us and calls us back to places of remembrance when we have wandered off the path. As my Dad puts it, "Traditionalism binds us to the human condition and allows no further development or expansion of experiencing God. However, tradition connects us to the faith of the saints and allows us to experience and enjoy the glory of God's expression of love."[66] The "AND" is what we are missing. We can do all of the things on the checklist and still miss out on the daily opportunity to co-create, to "Wait for the Lord," and to actively engage in inviting Him to direct our paths and sit on our front porch. To be clear, the results of this commitment do not always end with the best job as society sees it, the biggest house, the provision of what we think we want, or even the work we thought we were meant to do. It also doesn't mean that the people around us, including

---

[66] Rev. Charles Spraker, father of the author.

family and friends, may understand why we are doing what we are doing. It is quite likely that we will spend a considerable portion of our days misunderstood. To truly submit to lasting Front Porch Architecture that connects to the Heavenly Front Porch every day means to accept, not just acknowledge but accept, that His ways are not our ways.[67]

What does this acceptance look like? It means continuing in a role that has been assigned to us when the impact may mean fewer resources than we could have if we did something else and a family that is not happy about that. It may mean taking a stand at work or in a volunteer role that is unpopular but that holds the space open for change to occur in ways that most others are incapable of seeing at the time. It means recognizing that you could lose things that are of value to you along the way - friends that can't walk a more difficult path with you, enjoyable associates who participate in activities that distract time away from fulfilling your calling, time with family in order to be somewhere else to complete the mission, not having children because that is not a part of your calling, or simply being alone when you'd like to be included.

Being called to fulfill your role sometimes means being called away even while being called to something. In order to start being in a design phase, we have to pay attention and invest the time for our front porch not to be empty. As my Mom puts it, "I decided instead of worrying about the outside to spend time working on the inside."[68] It's the most important investment with the highest ROI we can ever have in our lives to decide that we are going to be connected, earthly to Heavenly Front Porch, and that our life is going to be a prayer.[69] The ritual of our doing can lead to a state of being, but if we don't know that something is supposed to come after the

---

[67] Isaiah 55:8, New International Version
[68] Marceil H. Spraker, mother of the author
[69] Rev. Charles Spraker, father of the author

doing, we completely miss out on the design stage for our lives. We remain incomplete. We think the doing *is* the end when it's simply a means that should carry us to another state with our chairs touching on the front porch, feeling the firm grip on the back of ours, knowing that He has got us, and secure in the knowledge that we're meant to stay on the front porch.

For me, this book is about being connected to the Heavenly Front Porch. I could have written a technical book for my profession. It would have been easier to whip out with decades of experience and illustrations to share. None of them would have required me to be vulnerable with the messiness of my own life story or to risk being judged or ridiculed. I could have cloaked who I am becoming. But this book was the test of obedience. This was about living my values and not from ego. This is the one I called in prayer friends to pray for regarding content and my courage to write it. This is the one that opens the door for you, soul-to-soul and earthly front porch to Heavenly Front Porch. If I wasn't willing to go there with my stories and the work I've done, you might not have the courage to do your own work, to start living on the front porch, and to be present to the good work that was prepared in advance for you to do.[70] I would have been accountable for failure to be obedient and for following my own ego instead of co-creating a template for others to pull up their chairs a little closer on the front porch.

So now, I extend a personal invitation to you to step up onto the front porch, dust off the chair with your name on it, apply a fresh coat of paint if it has gotten a little rusty, and let the arms touch. Enter into the phase of your life when you co-create with the Great Architect to construct the front porch that is meant to house you, your work, and your life in all of its magnificence as it has been planned. I invite you to connect your front porch and tether it

---

[70] Ephesians 2:10, New International Version

with filaments that you bind into a strong rope to the Heavenly Front Porch. Draw up the blueprints with an open heart, a willing mind, and in the presence of the One who has "engraved you on the palms of my hands."[71]

This is your space, set aside just for you, to continue creating the new design for your life. I invite you to be bold and courageous. Consider what patterns you want to break. Let go. Allow yourself to dream about living the life that you have in your heart but with which you have not connected fully. Ask God how He wants to use you and listen for His guidance. Know that whatever plan He has for you is greater than anything that you could ever dream of or create in solitude. Start taking baby steps down the path that leads to a full front porch life. Replace fear with faith. Connect your earthly front porch to the Heavenly Front Porch. Use your ritual of doing, beyond repeated actions, to lead you to a state of being, and experience your soul at its highest level of performance and its deepest level of connection.

Review the responses you have given to the questions in each chapter so far that have been leading you to the next series of Soul Sittin' below. Remember that the design is in constant renewal, so come back again and again. You may have to rest, get healthy, or get ready mentally, physically, emotionally, and spiritually before clarity is revealed. Time between assignments is not usually dead time but preparation time. Check in with the Heavenly Front Porch so that you have confidence in who is directing your path so that you can stay attuned, continuously being directed. Double check to make sure you are living out your values within His will and not your ego. Use the exercise below to bridge the Heavenly and earthly front porches in perpetuity and in alignment with the assignments that await your "Yes!"

---

[71] Isaiah 49:16, New International Version

SOUL SITTIN': DESIGNING YOUR FRONT PORCH WITH THE GREAT ARCHITECT

1. What is **God's will for my life**? When was the last time I asked Him? Let's stop and ask now.

2. What are **my dreams for my life**?

3. How have God's will and my dreams **inter-connected** so far?

4. As a child, when did I feel the **freest and the most in the flow**? When did what I was doing come most naturally to me?

5. Who do I want in my life? **Who is FOR me**? Who adds enrichment to my days? Who do I want standing at my funeral? Is there anyone I need to invite off my front porch?

6. How has God **used my life so far**?

7. What am I **feeding my mind, body, and spirit**?

8. What am I willing to **exchange in my lifestyle** to create a new depth of experience?

9. Where have I **not submitted in obedience to His will**, and how has that affected my life?

10. What do I need to **let go of** in order to step into the life He has for me?

11. When was the last time I prayed for His will to appear in my life and **meant AMEN** (let it be so)?

12. What is He placing **on my heart today**?

13. What am I **willing to commit** to doing in the construction of an earthly front porch on which I can stay seated for the next month, three months, six months, and a year?

14. What steps will I take tomorrow that will **demonstrate I am committing** to this plan? Next week?

15. Who am I **willing to share my design** with that will help me stay on the front porch?

16. What am I **most afraid of** in creating this plan? Pray for release from these blockages to staying on the front porch.

SOUL SITTIN' TIPS:

1. Write your prayer that you will return to each day during your front porch soul sittin' time that will reinforce your commitment, express and release your fears, and keep you sitting on the front porch in continuous co-creation.

2. Write a personal mission statement for your life. Focus less on what you do and more on who you *are*. Keep it close to you as well so you can stay centered in the way you are trying to *be*. (Add this to your "porch to Porch Plan" in Appendix A.)

    Author's personal mission statement example: *"I am a child of God, bringer of light, and a servant partner to seekers of transformed lives, enabling them to fulfill their callings to those whom they serve."*

3. Consider identifying scripture that speaks to the design on your life that will remind you of with Whom you journey and why you journey.

SOUL SITTIN' BLESSING FOR PERPETUAL DESIGN

"Stand at the crossroads and look; ask for the
ancient paths; ask where the good way is, and walk
in it, and you will find rest for your souls." [72]

I know you are a carpenter, but I struggle to sign up even as an apprentice for my own life. My front porch is dilapidated, and it often feels threatened as I flail through my days tired and unsure of my path. I haven't pulled up my chair as close on the front porch as I would like to be. I'm not even sure where my chair is at the moment, and I keep taking the front porch bypass going it on my own.

You have assured me that you still have a chair with my name on it and that you are ready to co-create beautiful new front porch architecture for my life. I'm out of practice with being available, and I'd like to experience a front porch homecoming at the table you've set for me.

---

[72] Jeremiah 6:16, New International Version

I'm ready for my front porch to be over-flowing, to let go, and to experience a cycle of rest and relaxation. I'm ready to know the blessings of the haven you provide for us.

I'm stopping now. I'm going to decorate my front porch for a royal visit. I promise to stay on the front porch and to do what is sometimes asking the impossible of me; I will wait for the call and live without fear in freedom through faith when it appears.

I know where I am now, and I'm turning to the Heavenly Front Porch, de-cluttering my life, simplifying, and listening. I'm ready to slow down to speed up and to walk in partnership with You and those family and friends You have selected to fill up my front porch. Until it's time to travel for the last time back home to the Heavenly Front Porch, I promise to keep the arms of our chairs touching and to rest assured that you have a firm grip on the back of my chair. Better yet, I'll keep this double rocker saved for us.

In Jesus' name,
Amen

Photo by kind permission of Andrea Dekker at AndreaDekker.com

"Commit your works to the Lord and your plans will be established." [73]

MOVING ONTO THE NEW FRONT PORCH

We can design all we want to, but unless we take the first step of action, our life's destiny will remain but a beautiful blueprint of the dream home that was never built with a front porch that was never full. Just like a move from home to home, there are steps to go through once the design is complete. Let's get ready to move onto the new front porch.

---

[73] Proverbs 16:3 English Standard Version

We don't want to take things with us that don't belong there. The floorboards are clean and have been sealed to protect against any difficult storms ahead. The banisters gleam with new paint. There is space for us to maneuver a large family or visitors when we want to be in community. The hooks are in the ceiling for beautiful hanging baskets to decorate this most special area. The front porch swing has been hung for some relaxation space. Small tables are placed around to hold cups of tea, journals, and budvases of flowers from the garden. A small nook juts into the wall for the banjo to lean into when its strings are dormant. Around the base of the porch, we've painted down to the cinderblock so that the porch looks like one continuous structure, solid in its ability to weather the future. Flowering bushes rest in trenches so that their roots firmly ground the soil to keep it from washing away and threatening the foundation. A bird feeder is nearby drawing in creation and the songs that remind us of a "morning (that) has broken like the first morning... God's re-creation of the new day."[74]

Into this sparkling environment where we are declaring the beginning of our new life, we bring with us what we choose. Just as you put together your moving to do list, put together your front porch moving in list. Go into your closets and pull out those things that will not be part of your new life. Decide what goes into donations for others who can take items on their journeys based on where they are going. You may have been a great soccer coach once, but that is now past as the children have grown up. Pass on all of your attire, coaching books, emails and referee materials to the next set of parents. The items that are assets that can be used responsibly on your new journey in a different form get moved to the keep pile. Get rid of everything else you are not taking in the

---

[74] "Morning Has Broken," *Songs of Praise*, 2nd edition, Eleanor Farjeon, 1931

yard sale or auction. Decide whether the funds generated can help to pay for the next degree, get donated to a charity of your choosing, assist you in forming a non-profit, or help you start that new business. Don't carry your old life with you onto the new front porch. It either has or has not served you well. Either way, you are intentionally moving into new space that is a product of who you are becoming, not who you have been.

In those same closets are other forms of baggage we want to leave behind on moving day, emotional, mental, and spiritual suitcases of stinky, smelly, laundry from trips made long ago. If it is not going to serve you well in your new life, why hang onto it or wash it? Let go of the hurts. Forgive, and allow yourself to move on. Those who have damaged you in the past have long since left on new journeys.

Give yourself the gift of healing, and cut the cord. Step into full freedom. If you don't stand on the front porch with both feet fully planted in your new life, it is a choice for which you have to take responsibility. Nobody is holding you to your old life. You may have to let go of some people as you step onto the porch. They do not include those to whom you have made a vow. Your moving day does include leaving behind those who seek to keep you tethered to issues, experiences, and relationships that serve them well but damage you, work to keep you from stepping into your mission, or are detractors instead of encouragers of your bravery.

Yes, it takes courage to move from the old front porch to the new front porch and to daily work to stay connected to the Heavenly Front Porch. If you take this on, it requires others around you to relate to you in a different way, because you are quite simply no longer the old you. Physically, you are located on a new front porch, and they have to decide whether they are going to cross the street to sit with you at your new address. Through no fault of your own, others may notice their dilapidated front porches and not appreciate being shown by virtue of your movement what they have chosen to ignore. Each one of us is in charge of the state of our front porches and the connections we choose to have. We can help each other to see. We can invite others to sit a spell with us, but ultimately, each person has to choose whether to keep their front porches connected.

Your moving day is a victory day for you. It marks the moment when you have chosen to map out a plan to keep your life connected, porch to Porch. If you've always been connected, your next plan simply allows you to add more filaments and make your anchoring rope even larger with firmer knots. If you have untied your rope, it's the day that you cast it back and anchor in again. If you've never felt connected, know that there has always been a filament that held onto you just as secure as if you had been space walking. You're just back inside the capsule now, knowing that you're headed home to your Heavenly Front Porch.

Know confidently that the Welcome Party is always there waiting for you. Know that the design is a co-creation of seeking, abiding, obeying, and executing, and you're never alone. There are always at least two rockers on the Heavenly Front Porch.

SOUL SITTIN': PRACTICING YOUR NEW LIFE:

1. **What practices** are you going to take with you onto your new front porch?

2. **Who** is going to sit with you **always**?

3. **Who** will you only allow to **visit**?

4. How are you **going to be** in your new life?

5. What will you **stop doing? Start doing**?

6. Who will you **stop being? Start being**?

7. What will people who know you **observe is different**?

8. What challenge do you have that you are not going to let stop you or not be an **excuse for failing to complete your mission**?

9. What do you need to **watch for on the perimeter** around your front porch that could threaten the new life you have declared?

10. What will **God notice is different**?

SOUL SITTIN' TIPS:

1. **Plan the move**: With all the precision and care of the most organized person you have ever met, write down a step-by-step plan of what you are going to commit to each day, as you get ready to begin residing on your new front porch.

2. **Time the move**: Give yourself plenty of time to create the plan. Allow yourself to have buyer's remorse for one day as you say goodbye to the journeys of the past, perhaps some people, and old habits. Set a realistic goal for when you are ready to be fully committed to what you have co-created.

3. **Set a day**: Name the day when you are declaring the beginning of your new life.

4. **Call in the right help**: Identify your champions, and make a list of them. Know whom you can call upon. God has placed guardian angels and people in our lives that assist us on our journey. He knows we need support and care. Along with prayer, allow those who are *for* you to help you prepare for

your transition, to walk with you through it, and to be your encouragers. Let them help you stay on the new front porch and to stay connected to the Heavenly Front Porch.

5. **Move**: Our actions, behaviors, attitudes, and habits, as we move towards and through each step, will define our ability to live out a front porch life that remains connected to the Heavenly Front Porch. We choose, by our actions or inaction. Step into being, moving, and connecting.

6. **Compose Your Declaration Day Statement:** As you step into your new life, write a statement for yourself that you can refer back to as you make this milestone. This is your declaration of a new life in Christ, the day of enacting your mission statement, and the beginning of living a calling. It deserves memorialization.

   Sample: Father, today is our day. I step out in faith and without fear as a child of God and your servant. You have called me to _____. I may not know everything about how we're going to fulfill this, but I am sitting on the front porch looking to the Heavenly Front Porch. I am committed, willing, and ready to live the life that you have planned for me. Today is day one of the Transformation. Let's begin.

SOUL SITTIN' BLESSING FOR MOVING DAY

"The old life is gone; a new life has begun!" [75]

I can't believe it's here! We've talked for so many months about where we are, the state of things, and mapped out where we're headed. Together, we wrote a plan. I'm working on both obedience and patience, and today, I'm making a declaration. This is the day, Lord. I'm standing in my new life with You. I'm not exactly sure how this is going to unfold, but I have confidence that my front porch is tethered with double-knots. You've put people, resources, and ideas before me that I can see are important in the next phase of the journey. I'm not sure how it all fits together, but I stand in full confidence, knowing that I am not alone. My front porch is ready for regular visits, and I'm committed to my new priorities. I know that this will be tested, and I am up to it. "I'll go where You want and do what You want, even if it's not someplace I think I want to be, if You'll just take my life and make something of it."

"May your front porch always be full and connected – porch to Porch!"

---

[75] 2 Corinthians 5:17, New Living Translation

Author's Parents: Charles & Marceil Spraker

"Behold, I have set before you an open door, which no one is able to shut." [76]

EPILOGUE: RETURNING TO THE HEAVENLY FRONT PORCH

"It will be just like going through a door." [77]

We all have stories of the near misses – the car accident avoided with a screeching swerve, the cushioned unexpected fall, the foot slip near the side of a mountain while hiking, the gasp for air as the lifeguard pulls us to safety, or the medical fight that was won despite the odds. As our hands tugged on the thin veil that didn't yield a permanent opening, we processed the moment with a "Whew! It's not my time."

[76] Revelation 3:8, English Standard Version
[77] Marceil H. Spraker, Director of Christian Education and mother of the author

We thank our guardian angels and God and keep moving into the next life moment, shaking off the realization that we were close to the veil becoming transparent.

Then, there are those existence-altering experiences that are shared by the world, magnified to an unfathomable theatrical stage by their very audacity to claim The Throne of control. On September 11, 2001, I was in Washington, D.C. with a colleague for an annual legislative conference. We watched the Pentagon burn. We watched people run panicked down the street. We watched the TV. We watched stunned people as we walked through the Mall trying to step off the cloying anxiety, the uncertainty, the fear, and the separation from our families. We stood alone in a silenced city where hummingbird wings could be heard. We stared in front of The Capitol as it glowed golden into the night sky as if someone had turned on every desk lamp and every strobe light inside and out, a reminder of hope and failure to seize control. We shared stories over dinner, expanding our conversations into more meaningful areas than we ever had, trading memories of what mattered to each of us, ignoring that this was an exercise in preparation for what may yet come to each of us and our families, and all the while in complete unspoken recognition that we were devoid of controlling the end game. We listened to our loved ones' voices with tones in them we had never heard before, knowing that it could be the last time we ever spoke. We watched the smoke rise above the pit that held the former World Trade Center buildings as we came out of the NYC train station, escaping back to the presumed safety of New England.

In that moment of catastrophic super-sized apocalyptic tears in the fabric of our world-view, we are reminded that we are never in control. Through the chaos, the anarchy, the missing puzzle pieces, and the seeming disconnected strands of our lives, there is meaning and sense, light and hope, purpose and path, and peace and love if we will but reach for it. The Throne is occupied, and the leadership is eternally stable.

One day, one of those near misses will become the final calling card of our entry into a new life on the Porch. None of us get a pass on taking the last journey. One of my favorite stories from being a preacher's kid comes from an interaction my mother had with a former parishioner. My parents were loved wherever they went, and former congregations have stayed in touch with them for decades. This particular man was middle-aged, and illness was bringing his life to an early end. He asked to come over and talk to Mom as he was dying. Of course, they sat on the front porch. Years later, Mom shared that they had discussed what the final journey was going to be like, and she said that she had told him that it was going to be just like going through a door. What is remarkable about this is not the analogy she used to help him prepare but what happened when he died. Mom received a call from his widow, and she said, "I don't know what you and he talked about when he came to visit, but I wanted to share with you what happened as he died." From his deathbed, the man said, "No, no that's not the door. There it is; no, that's not it either." And then a bit later, "There it is. *That's* the door."

Every day we awake may be the day that we push the veil back, grab the doorknob, and cross the threshold to the Heavenly Front Porch. Proverbs reminds us, "Blessed is the one who listens to me, watching daily at my gates, waiting beside my doors."[78] We are actively engaged every day in waiting beside the door that will open to us an eternal lifetime of sitting

---

[78] Proverbs 8:34, New International Version

permanently on the Porch. Each second we remain on the earthly porch is an opportunity to co-create in a space and time with our Creator, who promises, "I am the door. If anyone enters by me, he will be saved and will go in and out and find pasture."[79]

When you open the door on your Heavenly Porch birthday to eternally do some "Soul Sittin'" with God, how prepared are you to pull up your chair, so the arms touch The Throne, and to receive what the "eye hath not seen, nor ear heard, neither have entered into the heart of man, the things which God hath prepared for them that love him?"[80]

---

[79] John 10:0, New International Version
[80] 1 Corinthians 2: 9, King James Version by Relevance

APPENDIX A

"Forget the former things; do not dwell on the past. See I am doing a new thing!"[81]

SOUL SITTIN' VISION: MY PORCH TO PORCH PLAN

Years ago, my Mom gave me a picture for my wall that declares: "Your life is God's gift to you. What you do with your life is your gift to Him."[82]

---

[81] Isaiah 43: 18-19, New International Version

[82] The author is unidentified on the picture. Attributed to author Leo Buscaglia, 1924-1988 substituting "talent" for "life." Leo Buscaglia quotes at http://www.brainquote.com. Also attributed to Hans Urs von Balthasar, "What you are is God's gift to you. What you become is your gift to God." *Prayer*, http://www.goodreads.com.

Return to the porch often, and co-create with God as you rest assured that He has His hand on the back of your chair steadying you and connecting you to the Heavenly Front Porch. While I hope you will return to enjoy some of the stories occasionally to reassure you on your travels, use and copy the "porch to Porch Plan" template below to do some Soul Sittin' at any time in your life.

If you're moving into a new phase of life, stop for a sojourn on your journey to ask yourself a few questions about staying on track, and revisit where you're headed. Copy the pages as worksheets each quarter, as part of your annual New Year's preparation, or when you are considering altering your path. Kept that filament between the two front porches firmly attached as you work your way towards Home.

May your front porch always be full and connected – porch to Porch!!

My porch to Porch Plan

DATE: _____   NAME: _____

PERSONAL MISSION STATEMENT

Create a statement that reflects who you **ARE** and how you want to **BE** in your life.

Author's Personal Mission Statement Example: "I am a child of God, bringer of light, and a servant partner to seekers of transformed lives, enabling them to fulfill their callings to those whom they serve."

MY PERSONAL MISSION STATEMENT:

DECLARATION STATEMENT

The purpose of this statement is for you to define for yourself a commitment that you are making to how you have chosen to alter your life in partnership with your Creator. It requires four things:

To what are you committed?

What is the time frame by which you will start?

By when are you committing to completion? (If it is a state of perpetual behavior change, set dates for incremental improvement unless you are quitting a bad habit cold turkey.)

With whom will you share your declaration and invite to hold you accountable?

Example 1: **I acknowledge that how I earn a living does not seem to be in alignment with my talents, values, passion, or God's will for my life. I commit to seeking God's will for my work contributions, His calling on my life, and to begin researching how I might transition to a new professional life.**

Example 2: **I commit to transforming my life into one of listening for guidance, with patience and persistence, as I seek God's will for my life on a daily basis.** *(I will begin on Sunday of this week and am setting aside 15 minutes each morning as I start my day for prayer and Bible reading. I will share this declaration statement with my friend at work, whom I know is a person of strong faith, and ask for support as I seek God's will for my porch to Porch Plan.)*

MY DECLARATION STATEMENT:

FAITHFULNESS CHECK-INS

In order to stay on track with our plans, breaking down our commitments is much easier to accomplish if we do things in smaller segments. Refer to the end goal of your declaration and the time frame you have set. Work backwards from where you want to be, and list the steps you need to take to get there. Set a suggested target date for completing each step, and keep track of your faithfulness in moving towards full transformation. There are not a set number of declarations, commitments, or steps to take. Fill in as many, or as few, of steps "A"-"Z" as you need. This is your unique journey. Copy this table, or create your own, for more steps or multiple plans.

STEPS	MY ACTIONS	FAITHFULNESS DATE	FAITHFULLY COMPLETED DATE
A.			
B.			
C.			
D.			
E.			
F.			
G.			
H.			
I.			
J.			
K.			
L.			
M.			
N.			
O.			
P.			
Q			
R.			
S.			
T.			
U.			
V.			
W.			
X.			
Y.			
Z.			

FAITHFULNESS MILESTONES FOR CELEBRATION

In the rush of our lives and the checking off of our transformation attempts, we often forget to celebrate the progress we have made. If we're not standing at the finish line, we forget that there is value in the time invested in preparation and training for the marathon; that lessons are learned while we are on the journey to new lives, new understandings, and contributions of significant meaning to others.

Whether you are returning to review your plan again since yesterday, last week, last quarter, six months ago, or last New Year's Eve, stop and reflect on how you have moved forward in BEING your statement of declaration and living out your personal mission statement. Take the time to note the actions you have taken, the lives you have impacted, how you or those around you feel differently, the impact that has occurred, how others experience you, the new understandings you are operating from, and how these changes are impacting your plan revisions for the next period of faithfulness. Record the date so you can follow your own progress over time.

MY CELEBRATION MILESTONES:	DATE

OBSERVATIONS

As we begin a new endeavor to change our lives, our interactions with others, our goals, and our hearts, it is not unusual to notice that we may feel different. Others may react to us differently as we change – both good and bad. New people may arrive in our lives. New opportunities may present themselves. Others may go away. As you take steps forward in your transformation, it is worth noticing what is happening around you, how you feel, and how God is working in your life. You may have been de-sensitized from noticing for a long time, quite simply, because you weren't paying attention. Invest in noticing, and record what you are experiencing.

I AM NOTICING:	DATE

NEW UNDERSTANDINGS

As we spend more time connecting porch to Porch, our understandings of relationships, what is expected of us, how we feel about how we're living our lives, and what the next phases could bring, may change significantly. Use this area to keep track of how your perceptions may be revised about your life, its purpose, and where your journey is taking you as you co-design with your Great Architect partner.

I NOW UNDERSTAND:	DATE

SUCCESSES TO REPEAT

When we find ourselves in the exciting place of victories, the euphoria of the moment can mask the "how" of what led to our success. While we always want to thank God first for his provision and role in our progress, we also have the responsibility to make note of the resources, circumstances, people, preparation, and execution that led to the change, positive result, or new outcomes. Take some time to record what took place that led to any celebrations you may be recording so that you can identify what is repeatable in order to leverage the positives in your "porch to Porch Plan."

I WILL REPEAT:

EXPERIENCES TO AVOID

Through our attempts to transform, we also learn what should not be repeated, to whom we should no longer turn, resources that are not available, and environments we want eliminated from our life. Just as we should note what we wish to repeat, honestly recording what we do not want in our lives whether it be habits, people, locations, jobs, or temptations is an important step. Take the time to identify what is no longer serving you and could keep you, or lure you, off the porch.

I WILL AVOID:

BLESSINGS TO ACKNOWLEDGE

If we are living our life as a prayer,[83] each moment we are given is a blessing, because we are in full communion with our Creator even in the midst of our deepest pain, our greatest sin, and our darkest feelings of brokenness. If nothing can separate us from the love of God,[84] we are blessed. We can list our material blessings of daily food, gas for our car to get to work, clothes on our back, and a roof over our head. These are not to be taken for granted, but they are also not our greatest blessings. Remove the concept of material comfort as a blessing to keep this from being a simple exercise. Give some thought to what is currently in your life that is a deep blessing from the Source of your very existence.

---

[83] Rev. Charles Spraker, father of the author
[84] Romans 8:38-39, New International Version

I GIVE THANKS FOR MY LIFE'S BLESSINGS

PRAYERS FOR MY JOURNEY

As we declare new phases of our life, new journeys we wish to embark upon, and behaviors and practices we want to change, we must acknowledge what has not been in alignment with our Creator's design and has not served us well, in order to step into a new journey. We also have hopes, dreams, desires, and excitement about new paths, new beginnings, and yet to be realized futures that we want to share with our Creator. Go to your haven in nature, your home, or your place of worship, and author your prayers for your new journey. Sit on your porch and connect to the Porch, writing and sharing from your heart while you do some Soul Sittin'.

SOUL SITTIN' PRAYERS FOR MY JOURNEY

APPENDIX B

MY FRONT PORCH VISUAL

You've had a front porch you loved where your family or friends gather, or you've driven by one for years that spoke to you. You've seen photos of homes that have porches that make you wish you could own them and go there right now just to relax. We all know how we would fill up our porches. We have some version of who would be there with us and the adornments around us - the flowers and plants creating a haven of beauty, the cats, dogs, swings, rockers, books, magazines, bicycles, skateboards, fishing poles, garden implements, bird cages, games and toys, tables, tea cups, and comfy pillows. Visually, we know what represents God, peace, rest, fellowship, time, and filling us up.

This is your opportunity to design your own front porch. What would you visually design that speaks to you, creates a space for an ongoing life as a prayer, and brings you into full co-creation mode for your journey? Express your desire visually whether you have a front porch or not. Consider where you can create a porch haven in your environment that will encourage you to design and co-create often.

APPENDIX C

SOUL SITTIN' GUIDANCE FOR THE JOURNEY: RECONNECTING, RENEWING, RECREATING

Our lives are in constant evolution, and to remain enriched, co-creation must be an ongoing process. We don't craft our prayerful plans at high school graduation and then march forward porch to Porch never looking back. It's an ongoing conversation. We also don't live in isolation and need to incorporate those who will be impacted by our Soul Sittin' into prayerful conversation as well.

One of my favorite stories from a colleague occurred as he and his wife were leaving on their honeymoon. In the glow of post-wedding excitement while traveling to their destination, she had her head lying on his shoulder as the plane took off. In his most romantic of tones, he whispered, "Honey, what do you think the goals for the first year of our marriage should be?" She popped her head up and said, "You've got thirty minutes." When doing some Soul Sittin' with others, timing is everything!

Despite our best efforts, we allow our lives to plow ahead from activity to activity and responsibility to responsibility. Suddenly, we look up startled and wonder how we arrived at our current location, having no idea whether it's where our Creator wishes us to be or not. The only way to avoid that is to have a discipline of reconnection, renewal, and re-creation built into our lives.

Here are some examples of minimum milestones when you should consider returning to your "porch to Porch Plan" to do some Soul Sittin', first alone and then with those who are your journey partners:

Soul Sittin' as teenagers, high school graduates

Soul Sittin' after graduations and before embarking on the next phase of life

Soul Sittin' entering certification programs, tech school, college, or graduate school

Soul Sittin' at engagements, when newlyweds, annually, and at key anniversaries

Soul Sittin' before committing to parenthood

Soul Sittin' when founding a business, considering a new job, changing career paths

Soul Sittin' mid-career, mid-life, when empty-nesting

Soul Sittin' to plan business succession

Soul Sittin' to design retirement

Soul Sittin' for heading home to the Porch

For your convenience, and to encourage you to keep this book with you as a life resource, below are the questions from each chapter. Return to, copy, and reuse them over and over again along with the latest version of your "Soul Sittin' Vision: 'porch to Porch Plan'." God bless you on your co-creation journey.

SOUL SITTIN': TRAVELING FROM THE HEAVENLY FRONT PORCH

1. As a child, what **expectations** did you have of your life that you have lost?

2. What would it take to **recapture** your dreams?

3. What is the earliest story you can remember of **feeling connected** to the Heavenly Front Porch?

4. What can you point to that demonstrates your **awareness** that your life is a gift?

5. How are you **honoring the miracle** of your life and your Creator?

6. What immediately springs to your mind and your gut that is **out of alignment**? Personally? Professionally? Spiritually?

7. What do you believe the **purpose** of your life is up to this point?

8. What would the world be like **if you had not been born**? What would be missing? Who would be missing? What work would have gone undone?

9. Do you see your **purpose morphing** in any way in the future? What **evidence** can you point to for your assessment?

10. What are you **willing** to do to realign yourself with the Heavenly Front Porch expectations for your life?

11. If you choose not to fully step into your purpose for the rest of your life, what is likely to be left **undone** that could affect other people and their quality of life? What might you miss out on?

12. When are you willing to **begin**?

13. **Who** are you willing to tell you are beginning?

SOUL SITTIN': CREATING A LIFE OF FRONT PORCH HOMECOMINGS

1. What are the sounds, smells, stories, and memories that **evoke your ties** to the earthly front porch?

2. Who was present for you then – a teacher, friend's parent, grandparents, siblings, parents, pastor, sports coach, bus driver, or a Sunday school teacher? Who were your **shepherds**?

3. What do you miss from your childhood that you could **replicate** to keep those experiences, impressions, and groundings alive?

4. What are you doing now to **create a homecoming front porch experience** for your immediate family that will be their treasured memories and foundation for the future?

5. Is your **family more important** than work, soccer practice, cleaning house, or your virtual life?

6. What are you willing to give up to **be**, share, and enjoy together?

7. What have you done lately to let the people you love know you are **present** for and with them?

8. If someone in your immediate family died next week, what **regrets** would you have about the quality of the relationships that you have created with them on your family's front porch?

9. What memories reinforce your **connection to the Heavenly Front Porch** as a child? Even if you think you have always been disconnected, go deeper and think about walks in the woods, bicycle rides, playing on your own, reading a story at night, sitting on the beach, or feeling sad or lonely. When were there whispers from the Heavenly Front Porch even if you didn't have the language to express it?

SOUL SITTIN': FILLING UP YOUR FRONT PORCH

How you fill up the front porch of your life impacts the quality of every day and the state of your spirit. Give some consideration to:

1. If you have one now at your home, describe **your physical front porch**, patio, screened-in porch, balcony, or back deck as it exists now.
   a. What uses do you, your family, and friends make of this area?
   b. How would you like that to change?
   c. What would you physically add to this space to prepare it appropriately?
   d. What agreements do you need to make with others to embrace this area of your home, and how you would like them to connect to your porch?
2. On a scale of 1-5, with 5 being the most full, where would you describe the **state of your spirit** at the moment?
3. If you were offered 35 hours per week, or 5 hours per day, of your life back, is how you are living now, **how you would choose to spend it**? If not, what changes would you make? Add your alterations to your Soul Sittin' Vision: porch to Porch Plan. (Appendix A.)
4. Where are you placing **inappropriate priority** to your emails, Instagram, Twitter, Facebook, TV, on-line gaming, etc.?
5. What opportunities are you missing for God to show up in your life, or for you to show up in someone else's life, by the **behaviors you engage in that are drowning out your life**?
6. Where in your life can you **reclaim time**?

7. Where are you allowing others, besides God, to **direct your life**?

8. How often is the **Creator on your calendar**: Is it a mindless "time to go to church" once a week, or do you have time set aside each day to be with God? Is it a quick "Lord, could you take care of this, or is it a waiting and listening from Samuel's spirit of "Here I am?"[85] How empty has Jesus' calendar been on a daily basis?

SOUL SITTIN': SLOWING DOWN TO SPEED UP

As you continue to create your full front porch, address the following:

1. How, when, and how often, am I **inviting others** onto my front porch?

2. What relationships am I bypassing by **treating them as transactions** that are making me poor in life and cheating them from a full front porch life with me? Make a list of areas that need improvement, and next to it, write what you are going to practice to change your behaviors.

3. When was the last time you asked to be shown the **real work of your life**? What do you know it to be now?

4. Where, and with whom, am I **over-communicating and under-relating**? Is it with:

   a. My children?

   b. My spouse?

   c. My boss?

   d. My staff/employees?

---

[85] 1 Samuel 3:4, New International Version

e. My parents?

f. My friends?

How will I alter this behavior? What will others see as a result of this change?

5. How can I **slow down to speed up**?

6. Am I flying past God's front porch? If so, what do I need to do to **drive the heavenly speed limit** again?

7. To whom or to what do I need to start **saying, "No"**? What obligations can I reduce or eliminate and allow someone else to step into?

8. To what changes am I **willing to commit**: tomorrow, next week, next month? Are they permanent changes?

SOUL SITTIN': SIMPLIFYING AND LISTENING

1. What are my stories of how I have **reconnected** with the Heavenly Front Porch and then **renovated**?

2. What **journey have I not taken** yet that I need to go on?

3. How am I letting other people **junk up my front porch**?

4. What **weeds have grown up** in my life so much that I can't even see my front porch? What actions do I need to take to remove them?

5. Is my porch dilapidated with **callings that are no longer mine**?

6. Where do I need to trim back the hedges around my front porch, so I can see **how it connects to the Heavenly Front Porch**?

7. What is **holding me back** from living a full front porch life?

8. Where am I **setting time limits for God**?

9. What **new boundaries** do I need to establish to clean off my dilapidated front porch, so it's ready for the next calling?

10. Who is being used to provide **messages of reinforcement** to me regarding my path?

11. What does God have to say about the **state of my front porch**?

SOUL SITTIN': WALKING IN PARTNERSHIP WITH GOD, FAMILY, AND FRIENDS

1. Who has been walking the journey with you from the beginning that is **bridging the front porches** of your life?

2. What purpose do you **ascribe to their presence**?

3. What would be **different about your life** if they were not on the journey with you?

4. How are you **honoring** them in your life?

5. Who has surfaced at key moments and provided the guidance, counsel, nurturing, or direction that has **informed your spiritual journey** in the short-term?

6. Think through your life to date and find your stories of **being in God's community**, not just when people showed up on your front porch, but also **when has He had you show up on theirs**?

7. Whose front porch do you **need to show up** on now?

8. If someone from your front porch was unexpectedly and permanently **removed from your front porch,** how would you go forward?

9. Taking the time to be **more aware of your journey**, how will you interact with human beings differently from this point forward?

SOUL SITTIN': PREPARING TO SIT ON THE PORCH AND AT THE TABLE

1. What or whom am I holding onto that is **cluttering** my front porch?
2. When I let go of what I am clinging to, what is the **scope of possibility** that opens up in my life?
3. What **evidences of abundance** are present in my life now?
4. What **abundance could I create** if I de-cluttered my front porch?
5. How am I **limiting the options** in my life?
6. What am I willing to do to **open up my table** and accept an invitation to "sit for a spell?"
7. Who will I **invite** to my newly laid table with me?
8. What is my **timeframe** for laying the table and extending the invitations?
9. I have a **defined number of soul days** on the earthly front porch. What is the percentage of my remaining days am I willing to be stolen by leaving my table and chairs folded up on my front porch?

SOUL SITTIN': RECLAIMING YOUR LIFE'S NATURAL CYCLES

1. Where in your life have you allowed your schedule to negatively inform the **quality of your life**?
   a. What steps are you willing to take to **eliminate these effects**?

2. What is your body telling you about **how you are living your life**? Do you need to pay attention to
   a. Sleep
   b. Nutrition
   c. Exercise
   d. Noise in your surroundings
   e. Fun, play, diversions
   f. Health in general

3. Why have you neglected cycles of rest and celebration in your life?
   a. What do you **believe you are gaining**?
   b. What are you **sacrificing** by doing so now and in the future?

4. In the next month, how can you insure you have a weekly **period of rest** that involves only you?
   a. Who would be positively affected if you choose to **add this dimension** to your life more?
   b. Who can **join you** in regular attention to rejuvenation that will enrich your experience?

5. **Where is your life**: in spring, summer, winter, or fall? Describe why you selected this season.
   a. Spring: Bursting forth anew and incubating like a sponge
   b. Summer: Energetic robust activity

c.   Fall: Maturity, contribution, and meaning

d.   Winter: Blessing of gentle rest and front porch sitting

6.   **What season would you like** your life to be in now?

7.   How will you **deal with any disconnects** between where it is and where you want to move it towards?

8.   What will you gain by **sitting on the front porch** more regularly?

SOUL SITTIN': ASSESSING YOUR LOCATION - WHERE ARE YOU?

1.   When was the last time you **turned on the Heavenly radio**?

2.   What is **blocking you from receiving the signals** from the Porch?

3.   How can you **tune in the channel** for stronger reception?

4.   Can you **remember** the last time you were fully sitting on the Porch and what brought you there? What has changed?

5.   If you've been away from the Porch and returned, write **your story** of returning, and feel the **welcome home**.

6.   If you're on the Porch every day, what **practices** keep you there? Record them so that you can **intentionally** remain there for the rest of your life.

7.   Do you have only one foot on the Porch? If so, what are you willing to do to step onto the Porch and **sit in the chair with your name** on it? Write down some daily practices you are willing to undertake to move you onto the porch:

a.   I will **visualize stepping** onto the Porch and sitting down for a chat.

b. I will remove my earbuds at least once a day and **replace them with the signals from above** that will keep me connected with the Porch.

c. I will find time at least once a day to acknowledge that I need to **practice returning to the Porch** and to seek guidance on how to stay there.

8. Are you confident that there is a chair and that **you have an invitation**? If not, here is a simple prayer for you:

> Heavenly Father, I want to sit on the Porch with You. I know I have been away for some time and that You have patiently waited for my return. Thank you for saving me a seat and for having a chair with my name on it. I would like to sit down and rest for a spell with You. Please help me to sit in peace with You and to stay on the Porch, while I also have to live on the earthly one at the same time.

SOUL SITTIN': TURNING TOWARDS THE HEAVENLY FRONT PORCH

1. Consider your story. When have the legs of your chair been **wobbly on the Porch**?

2. How are you **prepared for your next response** when your front porch is attacked?

3. How will you **know that you are ready**?

4. What **behaviors and practices will you exhibit**?

5. Is there a shadow on your bench that is **preventing you from seeing the light** from the Porch?

a. **Where are you sitting** - on the lighted or shaded side of your front porch? We do get to choose.

    b. If you could **make one change** now in your choices, what would that be?

6. What may be **threatening your front porch** in the months ahead?

7. How will you **plan to remain strong**?

8. Are you under attack now? **What is at stake**?

9. **Who can you call** upon to strengthen you during this time?

10. Is there anything you should **walk away from now**?

SOUL SITTIN': LIVING UNDER HIS WING

1. Where are you sitting on the front porch? **Are you even on the front porch**?

2. How are you trusting you as the source and **living on perfectionism**?

3. Recall your stories of when you were **pulled onto the Porch** and provided protection.

    a. What did you learn?

    b. What won't you repeat?

4. When was the **last time you were scared** and had to rely on Him? How did it turn out?

5. Who has shown up and provided a haven for you, that was not a relative or a friend, and made you wonder where the **source of the help** was coming from?

6. What are you **feeding your mind, body, and spirit** that you are willing to give up to pull closer and live under His wing?

7. How can you **let go of your ego** and know that it's going to be more than OK?

8. How can you **spring into reverence instead of activity** next time you are faced with a crisis?

9. Describe what it **feels like when you are in His haven** and under His wings.

10. What **Porch boundaries** do you need to let Him set for you right now?

SOUL SITTIN': BEING WITHOUT FEAR IN FREEDOM THROUGH FAITH

1. **Replacing fear with faith** requires you to be in relationship with something. With whom are you in relationship?

2. What is the **source of your faith**?

3. How is your **life a prayer**?

4. Are you **going to the Porch before or after** you set out on your assignments?

5. Whose front porch have you not been on lately out of fear of rejection, pride, neglect, or past experiences with which you need to reconnect? Are you willing to shackle fear and commit to being the first one to **reach out in obedience and courage** to them?

6. Are you behind the glass like an animal in a zoo, observing the other side with **inertia or part of God's re-creation**? What will it take for you to **release yourself from the cage of fear**?

7. Are you **clinging to comfort** versus clinging to Him?

8. What is being **asked of you** that creates a blessing for others?

9. What do you **gain short term and long term** by staying where you are versus stepping out on faith?

10. What **blessings are you missing out on** as you restrain yourself from living fully and freely without fear?

SOUL SITTIN': RECOGNIZING & ACKNOWLEDGING THE HEAVENLY FRONT PORCH

1. When was your **last royal visit** and what was your experience?
2. What royal visits stand out in your life as **significant to your journey**?
3. If you've never had a royal visit, are you **open to receiving a Visitor**?
4. What do you need to do to **decorate** your front porch to receive a royal visit?
5. What do you need to **sweep out from your heart**?
6. What are you clinging to that could be **putting you in danger**?
7. Where are you on your earthly front porch? Do you need to **shift positions**?
8. What can you point to that indicates you are now **ready for a Royal Visit**?
9. What can you demonstrate that confirms your **readiness for the next assignment**?
10. If there are any **changes you need to make,** note them here.

SOUL SITTIN': WAITING FOR THE CALL

1. When was the last time you have done something for your family, friends, church, charity, or your work that you **knew was a calling**?
2. Think back through your life and record for yourself each time you have experienced a calling. Note **how you felt** in the moment, what you chose to do, and how you felt after your choices were made.

3. What is your **greatest regret** related to a calling? Did you not answer? Were you impatient? Did you leave the front porch?

4. Have your **forgiven yourself**? If not, do some soul sittin' and determine what you can do to rectify the matter, if it's possible now. If not, do some more soul sittin', and treat yourself as you would someone who was seeking your forgiveness. If you need to ask for Divine forgiveness as well, take some more time, and seek His comfort.

5. Are you hearing a calling on your life now? If so, where are you in **responding to it**? If you are pausing or ignoring it, identify for yourself why you are hesitating. Consider what you might be missing by not stepping into the role that is waiting for you.

6. If you believe that you have never felt a calling on your life, go through these four steps: **"Find your passion, know your values, pray for guidance, and live your dream."** When you wait patiently on the front porch, your dream will be His dream, and the alignment will fulfill you in a way that you could not create. That does not mean there won't be difficult times. It does mean that you have to remember the identity of your Boss.

SOUL SITTIN': DESIGNING YOUR FRONT PORCH WITH THE GREAT ARCHITECT

1. What is **God's will for my life**? When was the last time I asked Him? Let's stop and ask now.

2. What are **my dreams for my life**?

3. How have God's will and my dreams **inter-connected** so far?

4. As a child, when did I feel the **freest and the most in the flow**? When did what I was doing come most naturally to me?

5. Who do I want in my life? **Who is FOR me?** Who adds enrichment to my days? Who do I want standing at my funeral? Is there anyone I need to invite off my front porch?

6. How has God **used my life so far**?

7. What am I **feeding my mind, body, and spirit**?

8. What am I willing to **exchange in my lifestyle** to create a new depth of experience?

9. Where have I **not submitted in obedience to His will**, and how has that affected my life?

10. What do I need to **let go of** in order to step into the life He has for me?

11. When was the last time I prayed for His will to appear in my life and **meant AMEN** (let it be so)?

12. What is He placing **on my heart today**?

13. What am I **willing to commit** to doing in the construction of an earthly front porch on which I can stay seated for the next month, three months, six months, and a year?

14. What steps will I take tomorrow that will **demonstrate I am committing** to this plan? Next week?

15. Who am I **willing to share my design** with that will help me stay on the front porch?

16. What am I **most afraid of** in creating this plan? Pray for release from these blockages to staying on the front porch.

SOUL SITTIN': PRACTICING YOUR NEW LIFE

1. **What practices** are you going to take with you onto your new front porch?
2. **Who** is going to sit with you **always**?
3. **Who** will you only allow to **visit**?
4. How are you **going to be** in your new life?
5. What will you **stop doing**? **Start doing**?
6. Who will you **stop being**? **Start being**?
7. What will people who know you **observe is different**?
8. What challenge do you have that you are not going to let stop you or be an **excuse for failing to complete your mission**?
9. What do you need to **watch for on the perimeter** around your front porch that could threaten the new life you have declared?
10. What will **God notice is different**?

Author with her father, maternal Grandparents (Harold & Marceil Harris), & Great Aunt Lillian doing some early back porch sittin'

ACKNOWLEDGEMENTS

My life is the summary of thousands of people who have walked the journey with me and filled my earthly front porch to over-flowing through the chapters of my life. Below are but a few who specifically impacted the creation of this book.

God saw fit to provide two of the most God honoring, compassionate, gracious, humble, and people-oriented parents to have ever lived. For their introduction to God, love, wisdom, patience, guidance, encouragement, friendship, and forgiveness, I will always be grateful, as they are the biggest blessings with which a child can be gifted. Mom and Dad, Marceil and Charlie, you are loved more deeply than I could ever communicate. This book is an expression of what you taught me, as I've walked the journey of my life. Mom, there are no words to say what I see through Spirit in your eyes when we connect. I see God, my mother, and unconditional love – the love I know I will experience in person with The Father one day. Thank you for walking beside me each step of the way and for being my cheerleader. Dad, you are a man of God, my protector, teacher extraordinaire and father, who showed me God through your love, intellect, humor, teasing, sermons, and all-consuming compassion and care for human beings, particularly those most vulnerable. Thank you for introducing me to the recognition that my life is a prayer and for the lesson that Jesus didn't say, "Come." He said, "Go." Your love is a constant in my life that I rely on, now and always, an introduction to how God loves me.

To my grandparents, Granddad and Grandma Harris and Granddad and Grandma Spraker, I carry your love, lessons, poems, hymns, and stories with me, and I know you're watching from the Heavenly Front Porch. I look forward to sitting at the table with you again, and Grandma Spraker, I so hope heaven includes your cooking!

In life, the opportunity to have family sustain you, put up with you, forgive you, share with you, and challenge you is the gift that keeps on giving. To my husband, John, who has given me decades of his life as a partner and who has shown me what it means to be loving, I will always know that my life would never have become what it is now without the blessing of your presence each day. Thank you for loving me, standing by me, and helping me to learn how to smell the roses and do some "front porch sittin.'" You are my rock and the love of my life. To my stepchildren, grandchildren, and great grandchildren, you will never know how you have enriched my life by simply being there on my earthly front porch.

My dear friend, Henrietta, you arrived as Rosemary and Michelle departed. You know that your appearance was an intentional crossing of sisters from the Heavenly Front Porch. I'm so thankful for your love and support over many miles and many years and for your family (Ian, Camilla, Georgina, Hugo, Charles, Emma, Jane & Graham) that has blessed my life for decades. You're always in my heart, and I always look forward to the next time we can do some "soul sittin'" on the earthly front porch. I look forward to our next Evensong together. xxoo

My friend in forgiveness, Tracey, you are a fearless woman of God who lives *Heart to God, Hand to Man*[86] in an exemplary faithful, obedient, and steady way. Thank you for caring for our friendship and my family over many decades. Your presence in my life is a source of love, comfort, stability, and dependability. Your family IS family, and through them (Greg, Holly & Caleb, Will & Katherine, & Joanne) we have known the blessing of shared weddings, godchildren, holidays, and worship. I know we will have seats at the table together and will be joined as family porch to Porch.

I had the blessing of Dr. Billy O. Wireman, President of Queens College, as a mentor and second father in my life. We essentially adopted each other as extended family. Long after I had left college behind, we wrote to each other for 25 years until his death. His last lesson at his funeral reminded me how to live when he left his final thoughts regarding how he wanted to be remembered. A man, who touched thousands of lives and was a tremendously successful leader, humbly characterized himself as "an idealist with no illusions, who was called to obedience not to success," always remembering that he was a servant leader and

---

[86] The Salvation Army tagline, www.salvationarmyquincy.org

man of God. Billy continues to touch my life, and I know he is watching from the Heavenly Front Porch. Thank you, Billy, and thank you for bringing your precious Katie into our lives.

Dr. Cynthia Tyson, my friend of the same Christian name and fellow "Bringer of Light," you have demonstrated a life well-lived in faith that I have had the opportunity to observe since I was seventeen years old. Your hand has always been out-stretched to lift me up, connect me with the next step, and to hold tight when I needed it. While some people come into our lives and pass through it at key moments, you have been a constant, a friend of depth and of heart whom I treasure. Thank you for helping me through my journey and for encouraging me through these latest steps. You have my love.

Dave & Barbara Zerfoss, you are two of the most inspirational people in the world. Knowing you first as corporate CEO & marketing executive and continuing our friendship as you follow your passions to serve God by developing leaders and writing, you are a model for following God's will for your life. Great supporters, encouragers, and inspirers, thank you for nudging me along to follow my dream and for all of your wisdom and guidance. I'm unfolding my wings. God Bless!

Kelly and Matt Chandler, thank you for the gift of your lovely front porch and home as the scene for the author photo and website depictions. Kelly, you showed up as a friend in spirit, expanding our blessings when you found Matt and shared your beautiful life as Dylan arrived. Knowing you brings amazing people into our lives, including your treasured families. Thank you for the gifts of you. I look forward to seeing how your Soul Sittin' will continue to unveil God's path for your lives.

Nicholas Beamon, how do I say thank you for walking beside me as friend, colleague, and fellow believer, for shepherding me to the next phase of my professional life, for supporting my dreams, for challenging me to commit, and for reminding me to "keep hitting the note?" Thank you for saying, "Yes" to your calling, which in turn has blessed my life and so many others. God Bless you and your family, my friend!

Rhea Blanken, fellow follower of the God of Abraham, you have been a blessing upon my life through assignments God has given to me spanning two decades and to the thousands of people that the work has then impacted. You are a sustainer, creator, builder, and inspirer of hope. Thank you for standing in the light with me, my friend, for your faithfulness, encouragement, endurance, teaching, and love. Shalom with love to you and Bobby from us.

Gabriel Eckert, ye friend of many texts, how can I thank you for the constant inquiries on how this book was progressing, both encouraging me and reminding me that this was a focus and an intention to which I should remain dedicated? Your arrival in my life has been a source of inspiration and a constant raising of the bar. Yes, you are a respected colleague, and more importantly, a dear friend. Thank you for your generosity, your support, and your genius!

Robert Sumner, you have shared your faith, your life, and your family with me over three decades, as we have worked together to positively impact organizations and people. Thank you for being a point of light during dark times, for supporting my work, for teaching me, and for being a fellow traveler, friend, and believer. I have always known to whom I could turn for encouragement and Godly counsel as I have carried the responsibilities given to me. Thank you for your professionalism, precious friendship, and for sharing Jane and the family with us.

To my fellow C12 friends, thank you for a year of Godly friendship, wise counsel, and fellowship. This book became possible because of your advice to "slow down to speed up" and to keep the faith. Godspeed my friends, and may we meet again.

To those who have supported me on this journey or prayed for this book's creation and distribution, you have my deep respect and thanks for supporting me in this endeavor: Tracey McDanel, Sherrie Cathcart, Peggy Davidson, Ed Hickey, Linda Hamel, Dale Brown, Robert Sumner, Gabriel Eckert, Greg Martin, Kelly Chandler, Kris McBride, Christina Wilking, Becky Halstead, Nicholas Beamon, Beth Oleson, Barbara Zerfoss, Dave Zerfoss, Donna Gworek, Dave Swartzendruber, Buzz Leonard, Linda Hamel, Rhea Blanken and Shane Snively. Thank you for filling up my front porch and for keeping me connected porch to Porch.

To my partners at Westbow Publishing, including Edward Foggs, Adam Tinsley and Tim Fitch, thank you for believing in me and for shepherding me through the process of publishing my first book. It would not have been possible without your assistance each step of the way.

And to God, not last but first, the beginning and the end, my friend and my champion; thank you for providing souls from the Heavenly Front Porch to fill up my earthly front porch, as I have been ready to receive and as I have needed Your presence to be represented – sometimes to caution me, sometimes to correct me, sometimes to comfort me, sometimes to celebrate with me, and sometimes just to be. Thank You for the courage to walk with You when You answered my prayer of twenty-five years ago, *"I'll go where You want and do what You want, even if it's not somewhere I think I want to be, if You'll just take my life and make something of it."* My life has been more extraordinary than I could ever have dreamed or designed, and serving You is more exciting and humbling than I could ever have imagined. Thank You for helping me to replace fear with faith. My prayer for Your readers is that their front porches are always full on earth and in heaven. May You reach those You intended to touch with these words, my Lord and Savior, Father, Son, and Holy Ghost. Amen.

CYNTHIA MILLS, FASAE, CAE, CMC, CPC, CCRC

"Find your passion, know your values, pray
for guidance, live your dream."

Cynthia Marceil loves that she is named for her mom and grandmothers, connecting her to generations of women leading their families with faith. Discovering that "Cynthia" means "Bringer of Light" resonated deeply, especially the idea that as a willing conduit, possibility and hope could be brought into lives by connecting people to the light's Source. This book was received as a gift to share with those desiring to understand their place in the world and their relationship to a loving Creator.

As Founder of The Leaders' Haven consultancy, Cynthia is a business, servant, and soul partner to corporations, small businesses, boards, national and international organizations, and confidentially coached executives and CEOs. An international speaker, she earned an MA from the University of York, England as a Rotary International Ambassador Scholar and a dual BA from Queens College as a Presidential Scholar. Cynthia is a Certified Master, Professional, and Christian Coach, a Certified Association Executive, and an ASAE Fellow.

Contact the author for Soul Sittin' workshops, speaking, coaching or Leaders' Haven consultations: www.TheLeadersHaven.com, @TheLeadersHaven, or www.linkedin.com/in/leadershavenceo.

Printed in the United States
By Bookmasters